NEW

Angler's Mail

GUIDE TO

SEA FISHING

NEW
GUIDE TO
Angler's Mail

SEA FISHING

CHRIS CLARK

Consultant editor ROY WESTWOOD

HAMLYN

Acknowledgments

All photographs by Roy Westwood
Line artwork by Oxford Illustrators

Published in 1989
by The Hamlyn Publishing Group Limited
a division of The Octopus Publishing Group,
Michelin House, 81 Fulham Road, London SW3 6RB

Copyright © 1989 The Hamlyn Publishing Group Limited

ISBN 0 600 56354 5

Produced by Mandarin Offset
Printed in Hong Kong

Contents

FREEDOM OF THE SHORE

The irresistible call of the sea motivates many thousands to take up shore fishing every year and most get hooked for life. Recruitment is now running at record levels and when the North Sea cod are in reach it sometimes appears as though the whole East Coast is lit up at night from the Thames Estuary to the Wash. It is remarkable to see mile after mile of

If you are prepared to walk for your sport then you will find some magnificently wild beaches which rarely see a rod...just like this hidden, shingly cove in Dorset.

Cod are the main attraction and when the first battalions arrive in autumn many beaches twinkle like Blackpool illuminations all night long.

twinkling Tilley lamps vividly reflecting the huge upsurge in the sport's popularity. But when you consider what is on offer, the boom in British beach fishing is hardly surprising.

The prolific seas around our wild coastline contain a multitude of species and present the adventurous shore angler with a wide choice of target fish for most of the year. And there's not a penny to pay for the privilege of fishing among some of the most rugged and spectacular coastal scenery to be found anywhere in the world. No licences or permits are required to fish in saltwater and access remains unrestricted with the exception of a few isolated beaches which are privately owned.

The boom in beach fishing has coincided with something of a revolution in tackle design and performance. The old broom pole image which dogged sea fishing for decades has now been vigorously brushed aside by powerful carbon rods, lightweight graphite reels and chemically sharpened hooks. Shore fishing has matured from a game of chuck and chance into a much more technically advanced sport.

But it still remains relatively cheap to kit yourself out and compete with the best. In real terms the cost of beach tackle has fallen and it's possible to buy a complete outfit for well under £100. Just how much to invest ultimately depends on how seriously you want to get involved. The choice is yours.

Types of angler

Broadly, there are three main categories of shore angler each of whom has different perspectives on the sport.

Pleasure

The pleasure angler ranges in temperament from the fanatic who fishes every favourable night tide to the person who occasionally pops out for a couple of hours relaxation after work assuming he's lucky enough to live that close. Some are not happy unless they take home a bucket crammed with fish while others are content to catch a couple of flatties for the pot. But all pleasure anglers share the common bond of loving the freedom to fish where and when they like.

Club

The club angler takes his fishing more seriously and generally puts a great deal of effort into his sport. Many clubs stage regular competitions, outings and teach-ins for juniors. One of the chief benefits of contest fishing at this level is that the beginner has the opportunity to rub shoulders with experienced anglers who are usually willing to share their knowledge.

Match anglers

Most weekends there are scores of Open matches around our coasts, with entries for some of the larger, sponsored events exceeding 500. The match angler must invest a great deal of time collecting the best quality bait to maximise his chances of doing well against equally committed rivals. Nothing is left to chance and that means maintaining tackle in tip-top condition and building up a dossier on match venues well in advance.

Joining the Open match circuit is not a step to be taken lightly. It demands a great deal of travelling and expense with the likelihood of little return. Even the leading UK matchmen, who can earn several thousand pounds in a season, reckon profit is non-existent after all expenses have been met.

Probably the greatest satisfaction for the match angler comes from consistently winning competitions on unfamiliar venues where the fishing positions are predetermined by a draw before the match. These are known as pegged-down events.

Specimen hunters

The sea angling specimen hunter is a breed apart. He tends to be a loner and channels all his efforts into capturing heavyweights of a single species which he regards as the most challenging. Hard fighting fish like bass and mullet are among the chief attractions.

Success factors

Whatever category suits your approach, it is a fact that the thinking angler will always get more from the sport. Although it is possible to catch fish from the shore with inadequate tackle, crudity will not achieve consistent success. Quality bait and correct presentation count for everything. Nothing else will do if you want to catch fish on a regular basis.

I will be dealing with bait in the next chapter because I place it No.1 in the scale of priorities. After all, it's simple enough to walk into a tackle shop and find a satisfactory rod and reel but the same can't be said for bait. You'd be surprised just how many anglers restrict themselves by failing to appreciate this crucial lesson.

There are few creatures in Nature with the vibrant colours to compare with the male cuckoo wrasse which spends its life among the rocks.

Tidal influences

A thorough understanding of tides, the effect of their rise and fall, and of weather conditions on the feeding behaviour of different species is of fundamental importance when going sea fishing.

During each 24-hour cycle there are normally two high and two low tides. Exceptions to this include marks such as the Solent and Southampton Water where a peculiar tidal phenomenon results in a second high water in each tidal phase, usually one hour after the first high water.

A rising or flooding tide is known as a flood tide. As soon as it begins to fall again it is called the ebb tide.

When the whiting are around you certainly know it. Tapping on the rod top is virtually non-stop.

Highest and lowest tides

The height and fall of tides is determined by the gravitational pull of the moon and varies from day to day. The actual high tide time advances by approximately 55 minutes in each cycle. The highest tides in any month are described as springs and occur at the time of maximum gravitational pull when there is a full or new moon. At the other extreme, the smallest tides, known as neaps, fall midway through a moon phase when the moon and sun are pulling in opposing directions resulting in a weak gravitational effect and little movement in the tide. The interval between one high water and the next is about 12 hours 25 minutes.

Tide tables

Tide tables giving the precise times of high and low water are obtainable from local clubs and tackle shops. There are critical differences in these times even along comparatively short stretches of coast because headlands, sandbars, estuaries and other features can all substantially hinder the free passage of tidal flows. That makes it a good idea to obtain tables for those areas you intend fishing regularly as it avoids laborious calculations based on regional or Tower Bridge, London, charts. Mind you, these are reasonably simple to understand because all it involves is adding or subtracting the stated difference for your fishing patch from the high water times listed for the main centre.

The tide tables are normally set out in straight columns with the date on the extreme left followed by the high water time and height and the same information for low water reading across the page. Calculations are based on Greenwich Mean Time which means adding an hour to allow for British Summer Time.

Atmospheric pressure

Although it is the combined gravitational pull of the moon and sun which dictates tidal strength, the weather and atmospheric pressure can produce a tide that is far higher or lower than predicted by the tables.

Stormy periods normally coincide with very low atmospheric pressure resulting in tides which are several feet higher than the norm. This happens because there is far less pressure pushing the water out. On the other hand, low water periods hardly occur, especially when there is a neap tide and low pressure combined with a south-westerly gale.

Calm weather is associated with high atmospheric conditions and then you can expect some exceptionally low tides. These can be a real bonus for the bait digger as prolific worm beds which are rarely uncovered by normal tides are left exposed. High pressure also affects the flooding tide, holding back the water and resulting in a tide several feet below the expected level.

Feeding times and tides

The movement and feeding of various fish is inexorably linked to the different phases of the tide and weather patterns. Generally, a young flood tide is the prime fishing time especially on a shallow beach where there is a large rise and fall of tide. As the water starts to flood back over the sand, flatfish move in and feed on small crabs, worms and shrimps dislodged by the in-rushing tide. The fish will often chase their prey to within a few feet of the water's edge.

Many species feed most heartily in the fiercest of tidal flows. This is certainly the case with cod, smoothhound, bass, whiting and even the humble dab. It follows that the stronger the tide, the more food items are ripped from the seabed and carried along to the waiting fish.

Although a flooding tide through to high water is the peak feeding time for many species, there are a few localised exceptions. These are chiefly in areas renowned for experiencing strong tidal flows on the ebb but very little movement on the flood.

Feeding habits and weather

Different types of weather tend to control how fish actually detect their food. Sometimes scent is the most important factor, at other times the fish will find morsels by sight. But far more significantly, the weather largely determines whether the fish will feed close-in or at long range calling for a powerful pendulum cast and streamlined, clipped-down rig to achieve the necessary distance.

During settled spells in summer when the sea is flat calm and clear, many fish feed by sight and stay in deeper water making the angler's task more difficult. They can become extremely finicky and bait presentation is then even more critical.

But stormy weather gives the beach angler a real break! Fish move close inshore to gorge on the free harvest of food disturbed by the turbulent wave action and caution is thrown to the winds. Storms also allow the bait collector to stock up with the many shellfish which get washed ashore including razorfish, slipper limpet and cockles.

Discoloured water forces the fish to feed by scent rather than by sight and they become easy pickings at close range.

All kinds of marks

The coastline around the British Isles provides every imaginable kind of fish habitat. There are towering cliffs with deep drop-offs where sharks patrol, foaming storm beaches, eddying estuaries and rugged rock zones hiding mighty conger eels. Each type of mark has its own brand of attraction. Let us look at the main categories of habitats.

Sandy beaches

These might look flat and uninteresting but they're home for a wide variety of species. Bass are the No. 1 quarry from many southwest-facing storm beaches. When the sea is whipped up into a terrifying cauldron by gales, these silver kings of the sea feed in the surf, often just behind the second breaker and within comfortable casting range of any angler.

Plaice and flounders are the chief summer catch from many sandy beaches on day tides while night sessions are almost guaranteed to produce nocturnal sole on fresh ragworm. In winter, shoals of cod and whiting move in – particularly along the east coast – and the dab swap places with the plaice and sole. Lug and ragworm are probably the top baits for sandy beaches but sandeel and peeler crab also score heavily.

Power casting from rocks on a flat calm sea to reach bigger fish in deeper water.

Estuaries

The shelter of an estuary provides the angler with a refuge whatever the weather on the open sea. Flounders are the mainstay of sport for much of the year and in summer there's the chance of eels, mullet or even smoothhound. Coalfish provide extra entertainment at northern venues.

Ballan wrasse bite hard but spit out the bait or run you into kelp incredibly quickly. Even the tiddlers bend a float rod until it creaks!

Piers cast a spell on the young and old alike offering a safe, comfortable platform for fishing.

Estuaries can be muddy, dangerous places and great care should be taken because of unmarked quicksands and other hazards. For the bait digger, estuaries are treasured territory as they often hold huge beds of worms.

Shingle

Flat shingle beaches invariably produce similar results to sandy shorelines. Once the tide starts to ebb, you will find the shingle more often than not gives way to a sandy bottom. The basic difference between many shingle and sandy beaches is the strength of the tidal flow. Shingle beaches are exposed to faster torrents and that produces superior fishing in winter for codling and whiting.

Rock

There are areas of rocky foreshore where the seabed is actually relatively clear with sandy patches but often the rocks extend out for some distance with the additional complication of heavy kelp beds. Heavy tackle is a must. Species which prefer this rough terrain include wrasse, conger, rockling and pollack. Rocky marks which give way to broken ground are easier to fish and they hold a greater number of species, with rays, dogfish and cod frequently putting in an appearance.

Steep shelving

The 16 miles of shingle that make up the mighty Chesil Bank in Dorset is probably the best known example of a steep shelving beach. These deep water marks undoubtedly offer the best chance of a record catch or an outsize fish more usually associated with boat fishing. Turbot, ling, bull huss, rays and Trigger fish have all figured in the action at Chesil.

For sheer variety the steep shingle beach takes some beating. Normally, long range casting is not necessary with deep water almost under your feet but Chesil defies the trend. It consistently produces better catches of dabs, plaice and codling to those who cast the furthest. But when the water is rough and dirty Chesil responds to short casts like anywhere else.

Piers, groynes and harbours

The numerous Victorian piers, groynes and harbour walls protruding from our coastline again give the shore angler the advantage of reaching deep water with minimum casting effort. They are excellent, safe marks for novices of all ages to learn the ropes. In summer the strong currents around many of these man-made structures make light line floatfishing a superb method for many species. These include fish such as mackerel, garfish, scad, pollack and mullet.

Rich and poor marks

There are marked differences in both the size and variety of catches around the coastline. Some areas, like the West Country, produce outstanding catches and torrents of specimen fish while others offer meagre sport by comparison. This unequal distribution is basically brought about by three main factors – water temperature, tidal flows and most importantly the food chain.

Bountiful catches are commonplace in the south western approaches where the warm waters of the Gulf Stream lap the coastline. The abundance of wrecks and reefs provide the ideal territory for fish to breed and grow. Although many tend to be creatures of the deep, some inevitably find their way closer inshore to the benefit of the beach angler.

But there are a handful of marks – not exclusively confined to the South West –where giant fish, such as cod in the 40lb class, feature strongly. Without exception, these super marks are very deep with strong currents and have an abundance of food. There are often converging tides stirring up the bottom and releasing masses of food.

The beach angler's year

A typical beach angler's year varies from region to region although the geographical differences in fish distribution at key stages of the season are governed by similar patterns. Seasonal and weather fluctuations along with annual fish migrations and spawning rituals all have their effect on catches and must be taken into account.

The average year for many South Coast anglers starts with excellent cod, whiting and dab fishing during January. Flounders are in prime condition and full of roe in marsh and estuary channels.

February sees many flounders streaming out to the open sea for spawning. Cod also start moving into deeper water to prey on the huge sprat shoals which congregate along much of the South Coast at this time of the year.

March is often a lean month with only rockling and small flounders showing in numbers. But the odd lunker cod can never be ruled out and a few bass are also in reach as they feed on spawning ragworm in estuaries.

The first plaice make their appearance in April especially at deep-water marks like Chesil. The flounders flood back during May although many are in poor condition after the rigours of spawning.

June heralds the arrival of the summer species as water temperatures start to rise. Wrasse, smoothhound, plaice, dabs and bass are all on the inshore grounds. Mackerel should also be around, closely shadowed by large predators like rays, conger and tope.

July and August produce a similar pattern with many anglers turning to light line tactics for mullet, mackerel, garfish, scad and pollack.

September and October are the peak months for the shore angler. Many summer fish are still being caught as the first of the winter species start to arrive. This is a great period for specimen sole fishing at many South Coast marks and good sized wrasse and conger are also there to be caught.

The first blast of winter in November will banish the last of the summer species to deeper water. Large shoals of whiting and cod replace them, together with dabs and quality flounders in the estuaries. The cod and whiting sport usually peaks during December but it can vary by several weeks depending on the weather. Dabs, rockling, coalfish and flounders can also be taken in numbers.

The deep, golden colours of autumn are a reminder that fat flatties are gathering in their millions close inshore.

Species change with the seasons along our shoreline and that means there is seldom a dull moment. Chris met up with this green-eyed smoothhound in early September on the Chesil shingle bank in Dorset.

THE BASIC OUTFIT

This modest mound of tackle represents virtually all the gear I need to take on anything that swims around the British coastline. I always try to travel as light as possible.

1 11ft carp rod to get the maximum fun from mackerel, garfish and scad on light float tackle (Chapter 4).

2 Abu 9ft spinning rod for pollack, bass and coalfish (Chapter 4).

3 Full length chest waders. I find they're essential for fishing storm beaches when a big sea is running.

4 Miner's headlight for nightfishing. More versatile than static paraffin or petrol lamps which are no help when you are wading into the surf to grab a late night cod (Chapter 7).

5 Anchor pressure lamp used on the coldest of winter nights (Chapter 7).

6 A selection of reels.

7 Bulk spools of 10, 12, 15 and 25lb Maxima nylon (Chapter 3).

8 Filleting knife for gutting fish and cutting up bait (see Chapter 2).

9 Heavy duty rucksack for carrying tackle on long distance hikes to remote marks.

10 Cantilever box.

11 Bulk spool of 50lb Maxima for shock leaders, 60lb Daiwa mono for the main trace line and 25lb Sylcast which I use to tie up hook snoods (Chapter 3).

12 Home-made measuring stick to check that fish are sizeable according to local regulations (Chapter 6).

13 Groundsheet to prevent small items of tackle being lost in the sand or shingle.

14 Selection of weights including 5oz Breakaways, plain torpedoes, long tailed bombs and flat leads for rock fishing (Chapter 3).

15 Small cantilever box.

16 Strong gaff capable of beaching 40lb conger. A cord on the handle is looped around the wrist to stop a powerful fish wrenching away the gaff.

17 Landing net for use when floatfishing from rocks and groynes (Chapter 7).

18 Rig wallets to store terminal rigs (Chapter 4).

19 Brolly sheet to prevent wind and rain gusting under the sides (Chapter 6).

20 Zziplex 12ft, NG2 lightweight carbon beachcaster for bass and pollack fishing (Chapter 4).

21 Daiwa 12ft, high performance HPB-12M carbon beachcaster for lightweight match fishing (Chapter 4).

22 Zziplex 13ft, 2500M carbon beach-caster. This is my all-rounder and deals with most general fishing demands on the beach.

23 Zziplex Quatra match rod to tackle conger. I have cut 3in off the tip to beef it up.

24 Ian Golds Supermatch Tripod. This superb rod stand will take one or two rods.

REELS ON PARADE

1 DAM Quickfly 90 fly reel for mullet fishing with maggots.

2-4 Daiwa Millionaire 6HM multipliers with the level winds removed. They are loaded with 10, 12 and 15lb Maxima plus 50 lb shock leaders for fishing sand and shingle marks.

5 Ryobi S320 heavy multiplier reel containing 20lb Maxima for ray and conger fishing over semi-rugged ground.

6 Daiwa Millionaire 6HM multiplier fitted with level wind and loaded with 25lb Maxima to cope with heavy weed.

7 Daiwa Millionaire 6HM with level wind removed. Filled with 18lb line and 50lb shock leader to help lift fish up the sides of breakwaters and harbour walls.

8 Ryobi two-speed TS4 fixed spool. Ideal for pollack and bass spinning with 12lb line.

9 Shakespeare Omni fixed spool loaded

10 Abu 7000 heavy duty multiplier takes 30lb line to deal chiefly with conger.

with 5lb line to floatfish for mackerel, wrasse, pollack and garfish.

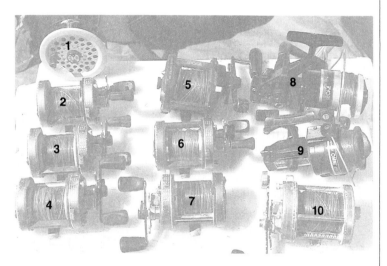

THREE-TIER CANTILEVER BOX

1 Mustad DC Easy Links, Aiken quick-change swivels and Taylor and Johnson Rapier split rings. All are used to connect rigs and sinkers (Chapter 3).

2 Sharp, surgical scissors to trim bait, flounder spoons (Chapter 7) and spare set of coasters to secure reel on rod (Chapter 4).

3 Beads used in the make-up of traces and as fish attractors (Chapter 3). Roll of knitting elastic to lash soft baits like crab on hook. Toothbrush for cleaning sand and grit from inside reels while on the beach.

4 Berkley heavy duty swivels and packet of size 2, gold coloured Mustad Aberdeen hooks used for flounder fishing.

5 Cox and Rawle Uptide, chemically sharpened hooks, size 2/0 to 7/0. Ideal crab hooks when cod fishing (Chapter 2).

6 Size 1/0 and 2/0 needle point Kamasan hooks used for dogfish and bass.

7 Small Berkley McMahon snap links to connect sinkers (Chapter 3).

8 Large McMahon snaps used for quick-release clips on traces.

9 Packets of size 1 and 2 Kamasan hooks. I use them as general-purpose patterns.

10 Selection of Mustad and Daiwa size 1 and 2 fine wire, Aberdeen hooks for flounders and dabs (Chapter 2).

11 Spade end, size 2 Mustad Limerick hooks with wide gape that are perfect for using peeler crab when eel fishing.

12 Mustad Limerick, size 3/0 and 1 eyed hooks. These are a fairly soft pattern and easily

bend out making them a good hook at marks where there's plenty of snags.

13 Baitsafe capsule to protect soft baits (Chapter 3), wire trace line, crimping pliers, screwdriver, roll of tape.

TWO-TIER CANTILEVER BOX

3 Dispenser of AAA split-shot to cock Drennan No. 4 Piker float (Chapter 7).

4 Plastic and stainless steel spoons for flounders and plaice, packets of size 14 Mustad, Dippa and Sundridge specimen-hooks used for mullet and small eels.

5 Wire booms to fish down the side of piers, assortment of Avon and stick floats for mullet, wrasse, mackerel and garfish in calm conditions.

6 Sundridge size 8 specimen hooks. Used as extra bait-securing hook in certain rigs (Chapter 2).

7 Lead bombs up to 2oz used when pollack fishing with spinning gear.

8 No. 4 split-shot for holding small bait on seabed, even when legering with heavy tackle.

9 Taylor and Johnson split-shot, small Avon floats.

10 My mainstay Drennan No. 4 Piker floats with several other larger floats, spools of Sundridge line and a handful of odd lures.

1 Breakaway lead lift to help keep lead high in water over rough ground and reduce tackle losses.

2 Bullet weights which I use occasionally when floatfishing in rough water. Plummet weight, with cork insert for hook, serves as depth finder alongside harbour walls and groynes.

HOOKS AND BAITS

Poor quality bait and inferior presentation are the twin scourges of shore fishing and that's why I make no apologies for promoting them in the running order of this book. Far too many anglers rush into tackle shops with a fistful of tenners in the belief that buying the latest, most technically advanced tackle will produce the goods. Frankly, they are deluding themselves.

Casting mania

While I'm parading what to some might come as unpalatable home truths, let us not forget beach angling's latest craze which I call casting mania.

It's now widely believed that cracking the 200 yard barrier with a lump of lead and line attached automatically puts fish in the bag. But more often than not the casting zealots are zooming their weights well over the heads of many species feeding close inshore. Too much effort and time is spent these days on tuning up tackle to improve casting performance before the basics have been mastered. If those same anglers invested as much effort into securing top quality bait then they would be well on the way to success.

Don't get me wrong – I am not condemning distance casting out of hand. Under certain conditions it is essential. But it will always remain secondary to the key issue of quality bait presentation.

Hook sizes and knots

Even fresh, succulent bait can be wasted through using the wrong pattern of hook. The diameter of the wire and gape size are among the salient design features which require careful matching with the bait and target species.

The majority of sea hooks are manufactured with eyed or spade-ends for attachment to the nylon hook trace or snood.

With an eyed hook, simply thread the line through and tie a half-blood knot. Trim the loose end of line with scissors or nail cutters to form as neat a tying as possible.

The traditional spade-end knot is trickier to tie, but persevere as this style of hook is a must for small crab baits.

The size range of sea hooks is very extensive but most demands will be met between a small size 4 and a 7/0 which is the largest a beach angler is ever likely to use.

Popular hook patterns

Hooks are relatively cheap and you should tie up new ones for every trip with the exception of large, stainless steel conger hooks which can be sharpened and used again. There are four leading patterns: Aberdeen, Limerick, Uptide and O'Shaughnessy. Within each of these classifications there are significant differences between competing brands. To avoid any confusion here are my precise recommendations for each pattern.

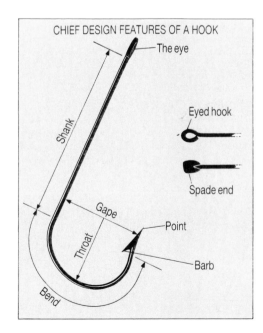

CHIEF DESIGN FEATURES OF A HOOK
The eye
Shank
Eyed hook
Gape
Point
Throat
Spade end
Barb
Bend

Aberdeens

I use two types of Aberdeen, the traditional fine wire versions and the more robust patterns sold under the Kamasan label. My preference in the fine wire Aberdeens are the Mustad 3262 and Daiwa pattern. But I rarely use anything over a size 1 in this group because the fine wire bends easily on a decent fish. The problem is magnified in the larger sizes which have a fairly wide gape.

A small size 4 or 2 fine wire Aberdeen is ideal when fishing for dabs, sole, flounders and pout. The Aberdeen's long shank and fine wire is perfectly suited to top flattie baits like small, fragile harbour ragworm but they need to be threaded on with care otherwise they'll disintegrate. Both the Mustad and Daiwa versions have extremely sharp points and prominent barbs giving excellent penetration and holding powers. Kamasan long shank Aberdeens with their chemically sharpened needle points are slightly thicker in the wire and are much stronger than standard patterns. They are the hook to trust at venues where there is a chance of picking up a weighty fish. Although the Kamasan barb is less pronounced than on fine wire Aberdeens, the thicker wire makes it more difficult to thread on small worms.

Limericks

The Mustad Limerick is a wide gape, short shank hook which teams well with small peeler crab baits when fishing for the likes of eels and pouts. This design of hook is needed with a bulky crab bait which would tend to slide down a long shank hook and mask the point. If the long shank hook had a narrow gape as well, then the problems would be compounded leading to

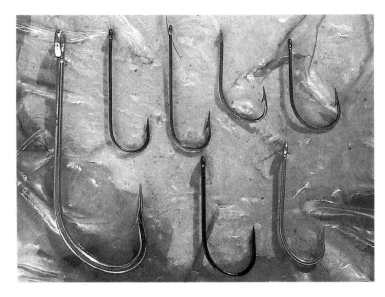

poor penetration.

The short shank Limerick allows the top half of the crab to be lashed securely in position with knitting elastic to prevent it sliding down and clogging the gape. But even if the crab did slide you would still be fishing effectively – it would not completely shroud the point because of the generously wide gape.

The Mustad Limerick is obtainable in eyed or spade-ends, but the eyed hook is made from relatively soft wire and bends easily. I much prefer the spade-end which is stronger and the ideal all-rounder for small crab baits. Whichever Limerick you choose, I would not recommend using sizes above 2/0. I normally stick to size 4 and 2.

Hooks to Trust. If conger are in your sights then you will require the big O'Shaughnessy hook on the left. The other patterns in the top row are a Kamasan Aberdeen, traditional fine-wire Aberdeen and Mustad-eyed and spade-end Limericks for crab baits. On the bottom row are a Cox and Rawle Uptide pattern and smaller stainless-steel O'Shaughnessy.

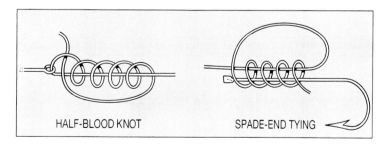

HALF-BLOOD KNOT   SPADE-END TYING

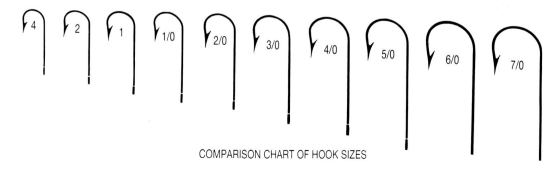

COMPARISON CHART OF HOOK SIZES

Freshly dug ragworm look sturdy but the tail end is brittle.

Uptide

A more robust hook is necessary for larger crab baits when after cod, smoothhound and bass. The Cox and Rawle high tensile Uptide pattern fits the bill. This wide gape, short shank hook is extremely strong even in the larger sizes. The 3/0 and 5/0 are cracking hooks to use with big crab baits when the cod are running.

O'Shaughnessy

The O'Shaughnessy design is an extremely strong hook made from stainless steel with a medium length shank and average size gape. My preferred patterns in this range are the Mustad 34007 and Daiwa Superstrike. It's the hook to use for powerful fish in rocks or kelp as it will withstand considerable punishment.

I use the Mustad in a size 1 for wrasse. I've never had one of these hooks bend out of shape even when a large fish has got me stuck solid in kelp.

The Daiwa Superstrikes in sizes 5/0 and 7/0 are my trusted conger irons. The hook is 100 per cent reliable, with a razor sharp point. That is important because conger are often finicky feeders.

Bait categories

The natural diet of sea fish consists chiefly of worms, small prey fish and shellfish. In bright, clear conditions fish usually feed largely by sight and are more inclined to take prawns, sandeels and crabs. When the water is rough and coloured, scent plays a major part in food location and shellfish, worms and peeler crab are more readily taken.

It is virtually always essential that the bait is fresh but there are some, such as slipper limpet, which work better if they are a few days old.

Versatile worms

Of all the natural baits, worms will be accepted regardless of weather conditions and they rate as the most prolific catchers of sea fish because they figure so prominently in their diet. Professional bait-diggers earn their living supplying tackle shops with vast quantities of rag and lug but quality is variable the further you go inland.

RAGWORM

The common red ragworm with its distinctive, centipede-like paddles running along both sides of its body serves as nourishment for a wide range of species. It is carnivorous and feeds on small invertebrates and other tiny particles that it filters from mud, shingle or fine sand. Normally, only the giant king ragworm, which can grow to several feet in length, are found in sand with the smaller worms preferring mud or shingle.

It is worth pointing out that worms dug from mud keep better than shingle rag and they're a far firmer bait, probably because they are not so watery. Collecting ragworm is a back-aching task especially in winter when they burrow deeper to escape the cold. Invest in a wide-pronged potato fork if you intend digging your own and that will eliminate a lot of the sweat.

It is relatively simple to locate the most prolific areas of worms. Walk carefully across the mud keeping an eye open for little jets of water squirting from small holes. That's a sure sign that ragworm are in residence and then it's just a case of digging where there is the greatest density of worms.

Ragworm should always be handled with care. Grip them near the head as the tail end is brittle and breaks easily. Also these worms can inflict a nasty bite with powerful, horny-like nippers which protrude from the jaw. It's not unknown for them to draw blood.

Obtaining supplies of top quality ragworm is always difficult if you live well inland but the future looks more bright now that farm-reared ragworm are becoming available. Increasing demand for rag is inevitably imposing heavy pressures on bait beds. Next time you are bait digging remember that fact, spare a thought for the next generation of anglers and only take sufficient for your needs. Without conservation, ragworm stocks could dwindle rapidly.

Over the years, I've found that ragworms of 5-6in produce the best results. I would sooner use half-a-dozen small rag with lots of tails dangling attractively from the hook than a single, big worm. The only time I favour the intimidating giant king rag is when smoothhound and stingray fishing at western Solent beaches or for general ray fishing.

Mounting rag on the hook

Ragworm should be threaded on the hook head first. Feed the hook through the body, gently drawing the worm around the bend, up the shank and past the eye until the tail is left hanging free below the barb. The only exception to this method is for sole living on muddy bottoms. For reasons I've never fathomed they want their rag threaded on tail first with the head around the point of the hook.

Storage techniques

It's possible to store ragworm in a tank of aerated sea water and many anglers find this a satisfactory method. The water must be kept cool and any dead worms removed immediately. Tanked rag are best taken from the water 24 hours before you intend using them and left to dry on newspaper. But I've got to admit that I regard this technique as inferior to storing worms in a fridge. Untanked rag make a much better bait.

My system of storing rag is to lay the worms in trays lined with newspaper and

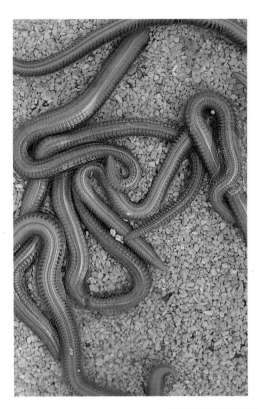

White rag will remain lively if they are stored in coral sand and sea water in the fridge.

Lugworm are the only bait worth using at many of the big cod marks.

Yellowtail lug – this bait is in short supply.

then cover them with seaweed. The trays are kept in a fridge with the temperature set between 40 – 45 degrees Fahrenheit. Freshly dug ragworm will remain in perfect condition for several weeks but if the temperature rises and they start to die there is little that can be done to save them. Never retain broken and whole worms together otherwise they will quickly deteriorate.

Transporting ragworm on short trips is easy with a covering of seaweed in a plastic bucket. But if you're travelling a long distance, a cool box will be needed.

Swimmers at spawning time

Ragworm swim to the surface in early spring to spawn. The males develop bright green spawning livery and after quitting their burrows at this time they are very soft, making them easy pickings. Bass, in particular, soon move inshore to gorge themselves on the free-swimming rag.

These green worms are of little use as hook bait from open beaches because they break up too easily. But they score well in estuaries, where fish are often stuffed full with spawning rag in spring.

WHITE RAGWORM

No angler worth his salt would enter a major competition without a supply of lively whites which are markedly different in appearance from red ragworm. In fact, they are not true ragworm at all and their colour varies from a pearly white, among the bigger specimens, to a dirty grey depending on the sand or gravel they frequent. All white rag have a pronounced vein running just under the skin from head to tail. They are ferocious cannibals which often kill red rag on sight.

Whites are extremely active and wriggle violently when handled, eventually forming tight coils or even breaking in half. They are so fast moving that a whole colony can shift several hundred yards overnight. Not for nothing are they known as snakes!

The exact location of many white rag beds is kept secret but areas of small stones or coarse sand containing a large population of tube worms are a favourite

habitat, especially if the sand is fairly wet. They like liquid sand because they can travel through it at a rate of knots searching for unsuspecting prey.

Large pearly white snakes can only be collected on a big spring tide. Look for a small ridge of coarse sand as close as possible to the low water mark. As a rule you do not have to dig too deeply to gather smaller whites because they live in the top 6 in. But the larger worms tend to be much deeper.

Average size whites can be dug on smaller tides but don't expect a bucketful. About 60 an hour would be good going but you would have to excavate getting on for a ton of spoil!

Smaller fish show a distinct liking for small, white ragworm on a fine wire, size 2 Aberdeen hook. Larger snakes are a superb cod bait and can be used singly on a size 2/0 Kamasan.

Storage techniques

White rag must be left in a bucket of sea water for 24 hours to clean themselves before being stored in the fridge. Never mix them with other types of worms or retain broken ones – they will quickly foul the water.

For best results, store in a fridge, on a tray containing coral sand and covered with 2in of fresh sea water, a maximum of ten worms to a tray. The fridge temperature should be set at 45 degrees Fahrenheit. In transit, pack the trays in a cool box after pouring away the sea water.

HARBOUR RAGWORM

Harbour rag look similar to normal red ragworm but there's a pronounced yellow vein running along the whole length of the body. This most delicate of all worm-baits seldom exceeds 3in. and is favoured by the match angler for snatching small fish. Their beds are found near the high tide mark in estuaries and harbours and they can be gathered on the smallest of neap tides.

It's possible to collect a dozen or more with a single forkful of mud or gravel and they will even live in brackish water.

Superb for flatties

A fine wire, whipped or spade-end hook is required to present these small worms, with a size 4 tied to a snood of 5-10lb nylon fitting the bill. Thread a dozen maddies up the line and you've got a superb flattie bait. The coffin-shaped Baitsafe device which holds the bait inside a chamber and then releases it on impact with the sea (see Chapter 3) is the perfect partner for delicate harbour rag as it prevents them disintegrating on the cast.

Maddies also produce bonus fish when used to tip off white ragworm. Simply thread a couple of maddies on the hook after it has been baited with whites and you've served up a potentially deadly cocktail.

Harbour rag mounted on a size 6 hook tied to 3lb line and fished behind a little silver spoon will turn the head of difficult mullet. If you try this method, hook the worms by their heads leaving the body to trail attractively in the tide.

Storage techniques

Storing maddies poses no problems. First wash them thoroughly in sea water as soon as you have finished digging. Then lay them on damp hessian or newspaper in trays and place them in a fridge set at 45 degrees Fahrenheit. They can also be retained in weed or an aerated tank.

LUGWORM

The popularity of lugworm puts most other sea baits in the shade. It is widely distributed and produces fish consistently, particularly at the country's big cod marks where it is often the only bait worth using. There are three categories of this worm classified as the common blow lug and the black and yellowtails.

BLOW LUGWORM

These are found in all types of terrain from sandy storm beaches to muddy estuaries. But it's the sandy venues which offer the easiest and most productive digging opportunities.

Blow lug live in a U-shaped burrow with a coiled cast of sand revealing their presence. Look carefully and you'll also see a small hole a few inches from the cast which is the other end of the worm's burrow. The casts are discharged by the lug as it filters the sand for food. They appear as the tide starts to ebb and the biggest concentration will be located at the low water line, especially on a big tide. This is also where the largest worms will be found.

A thin, wire type hook baited with four small lug is fine for plaice and whiting but cod demand slightly larger and stronger hooks with bigger worms.

Storage techniques

Once again a wide-pronged potato fork is the most efficient tool for digging up these worms in wet sand and mud. I normally drop freshly dug lugworm into a bucket of clean seawater, separating out any broken ones to avoid killing the lot.

I try to dig three days before the worms are actually required. I leave them in water for the first two days giving them time to wash through sand and debris in their system. Then I place the worms on a sheet of newspaper for 20 hours to dry. This hardens them up and results in a far better hookbait.

One additional tip, which will help keep your lug in the best condition, is to place

Shakespeare aerator and plastic bucket is just the job for keeping shrimps and sandeels alive.

damp hessian over them while they are laid out on newspaper.

Never keep blow lug in a hot room or direct sunlight otherwise they will do exactly what their name suggests and blow. A cool, darkened room or fridge set at 45 degrees Fahrenheit is the right climate.

BLACK AND YELLOWTAIL LUG

These worms come into their own for cod and will outfish blow lug every time. But their beds are extremely limited. Kent and North Wales hold the biggest stocks.

Unlike blow lug, these worms live in a burrow which goes straight down for several feet. Their casts also differ in that the coils of sand are completely symmetrical.

Yellowtails can be trench dug with a potato fork in summer on the Kent coast but a bait pump is a more practical solution for big black lug. The pump is pushed into the beach directly over a cast and, hopefully, sucks up the worm along with sand.

Storage techniques

Yellowtail lug will happily survive in tanks of water, twisting themselves into tight coils. But keep them cool and don't store too many in a container.

Another method of retaining yellowtail and black lug is to gut them as soon as they are dug by squeezing out all the sand from their insides. Wrapped individually in newspaper, they will keep for several days or can be frozen. Frozen black lug is a great bait for dabs at deep water marks like Chesil and Dungeness.

The crack along the side of the shell confirms this is a peeler crab.

Crabs

All crabs must shed their shells from time to time in order to grow and during the moulting period they give off a scent which acts as a powerful stimulant to fish. Crabs in this state are described as peelers.

Peelers

What actually happens during a moult is that the crab fills itself up with water forcing its shell to crack and fall off. The old claws and legs are also discarded leaving a soft, new green skin underneath which enlarges and takes several days to harden. When they are moulting or soft the crabs become lethargic and vulnerable to predators.

Edible crabs, the velvet swimming variety and common shore crabs are all of interest to the shore angler. But the velvet swimming crab is the hardest to obtain because of its preference for deep water.

How to recognise peelers

Peeler crabs shelter under boulders or along the edges of groynes and harbour walls, often burying themselves under the sand for extra protection. When they've actually shed their shells, the shore crabs cannot be mistaken for anything else but a softie because they are literally extremely soft to the touch. Peelers are less obvious but there are several tell-tale signs that the crab is in the process of a moult.

During the early part of the season, large cock crabs are the first to start discarding their shells. Old hands recognise these by the feel, colour and general appearance. Novices will almost certainly need to carry out a test to check if the crab is a peeler or not. This simply involves twisting and removing an end leg segment. If a soft, brightly coloured new skin is revealed underneath the old shell then it's definitely a peeler. But if white muscle and tissue is found then the crab is not moulting.

At an advanced stage of moulting, the crab's shell will start to split away, with a

crack appearing along the side of its body. These crabs are in prime condition for fishing. As a general rule, crabs that are a dull matt colour or covered in barnacles are more likely to be peelers.

In early summer, the smaller female crabs begin to moult. Some of these hide away in silt but more often than not they will be carried underneath a male. If the female is being carried the correct way up then the crab will be a peeler. But if it is carried upside down it will be a softie mating with the male crab above.

A second moult of the large cock crab occurs in autumn just before they move off into deeper water at the first hint of cold weather. Moulting periods are difficult to pinpoint precisely as they vary depending on weather conditions and water temperature.

Put boulders back

When searching for peelers on the shoreline, replace all rocks and stones exactly as they were found. If they are left upturned it will destroy the intertidal food chain for months and even crabs will stay away.

For your own protection, wear rubber gloves when crabbing to avoid getting your hands cut on sharp rocks and buried fragments of glass.

Storage techniques

Live peelers must be retained among weed in a fridge set at the mandatory

Peeler Presentation

Top left: Kill the crab before removing the legs and all traces of the shell.

Top: Cut away the gills.

Above: Cut body in two, mount on hook and lash tight with knitting elastic.

Left: Crab legs are tough and make a splendid bait in their own right.

45 degrees Fahrenheit. They should be checked daily and any dead ones re-

moved. Every second day, place them in saltwater for about one minute. That is just long enough for them to wet their gills without taking in too much water. This will ensure the peelers remain in first-class condition.

Mounting on the hook

Before mounting a crab on the hook, kill it as humanely as possible with a pointed tool. Lift away the top shell and remove the legs and claws. Strip off all the remaining shell including the bits around the mouth before cutting out the gills with scissors.

The crab is now ready to use, although it may need to be cut in half depending on its size and the type of fish you are seeking. The legs can be used on their own or for tipping off other baits once they've also been peeled to expose the new soft legs underneath.

The wide-gape, spade-end Limerick is ideal for smaller baits while the Cox and Rawle Uptider pattern is suited to larger mouthfuls. Lash the crab on the shank with knitting elastic if necessary, to help hold it in place during the rigours of the cast.

When fishing for smaller species I find half a crab is more than adequate. Cutting it in half allows the juices and scent to flow more freely. This also holds true when using a whole crab for cod, bass and smoothhound on a size 2/0 Cox and Rawle Uptider. I find catch rates are increased by cutting the crab three-quarters of the way through before threading it on the hook and whipping it with elastic thread.

One useful tip, particularly when smoothhound fishing is to tip off the bait with a couple of peeled legs. This certainly increases the catch rate. Peeled legs and claws are also effective for tipping off worm baits. They are rather tough and sinewy which prevents crabs stripping a bait too quickly.

Legs and claws catch fish in their own right. Half-a-dozen fished on a size 2 Aberdeen will produce plenty of small flounders, eels and pout. In fact, legs fished in this way often outfish a bulky crab bait for smaller species.

Freezing peelers

Strange as it may seem, correctly frozen peelers can yield better results than fresh baits. Frozen peelers release scent and juices far more quickly and that's often an advantage in a match.

The best time to freeze crabs is during the spring moult when a flush of big cock crabs peel simultaneously making collection easy. But crabs must be in prime moulting condition with the shell just starting to split away. Dead or hard crabs are totally useless for freezing.

Remove all the shell and the gills as already described. Failure to cut away the gills could turn the crab black and render it useless. Once the peeler has been completely cleaned, wash it in fresh water and then dry with paper kitchen towel. Wrap the crabs individually in clingfilm, making sure each packet is totally airtight, before placing them in the coldest part of the freezer on a flat tray. It's a good idea to date stamp each container. The legs and claws can also be frozen but keep them separate from the bodies.

Incidentally, tinfoil is not as good as clingfilm because it's difficult to get airtight and the crabs will eventually dry out making them less potent.

Transporting peelers

Frozen crabs must not be allowed to thaw out until just before they are needed as hookbait and should be transported in a large Thermos flask. Place the flask in the freezer the night before your trip to ensure the crabs travel in a perfect frozen state.

On the beach, remove no more than five or six peelers at any one time from the flask and tighten the lid immediately afterwards. Tipping out all the crabs at the start will make some of them useless as hookbaits before the session is finished.

HARDBACK CRABS

Surprisingly, anglers achieve very little success with hardback crabs even though they are regularly eaten by many inshore fish. The reason remains a mystery. Wrasse and smoothhound are the only two species which are enthusiastic about hardbacks presented on the hook. Small crabs about the size of a 10p piece work best but the presentation is critical.

Mounting hardbacks

First remove the claws before mounting the hardback by passing the hook through its body approximately half-an-inch from its jaw. There's no need to tie the crab with elastic thread unless you are distance casting. The O'Shaughnessy pattern rules supreme for wrasse and smoothhound when using hardbacks. Tie on a size 2 for wrasse and a 3/0 for smoothhound.

Storage techniques

Collect small hardbacks from any rough ground just below the high-water mark. Store them in a cool, darkened shed with a good covering of weed. Keep them well away from heat and direct sunlight. They will need a daily soaking in saltwater but the length of time they spend in the water is not important.

HERMIT CRABS

These make excellent baits for many species, including cod and smoothhound, although they are extremely soft and difficult to cast. Unlike other crabs, the hermit does not moult in order to grow. It lives in a vacant winkle or whelk shell and scouts around for a larger shell when it outgrows its current home.

Good-size hermits are not commonly found in the intertidal zone. The most effective way of collecting them is with a weighted dropnet baited with a piece of smelly fish and lowered from a pier, breakwater or harbour wall.

A small hammer is needed to crack the shell to release the hermit. But don't smash it too hard or you'll be left with a pulped crab. Apart from its main claw, the body of a hermit is too soft for distance casting. A 2/0 fine wire hook will hold these delicate baits and deal with a decent cod or smoothie.

Hermits must be retained in a cool, aerated tank of seawater. They won't survive for very long out of water and damp weed will only sustain them for a short period.

Prawns and shrimps

High sea temperatures in summer tempt prawns and shrimps inshore but they soon scurry back into deep water as colder weather begins to bite. The heaviest concentrations are usually in the vicinity of harbour walls, rocky outcrops and the base of seaweed covered piles.

Collecting these shellfish presents very few problems with a purpose-designed pushnet. As the tide ebbs away, the net is worked over rough ground or weed and apart from prawns you'll also catch a good number of small fish.

The alternative method is to use a dropnet baited with fish or meat. The net must have a top which closes as soon as it is lifted from alongside a pier or harbour wall otherwise the prawns will flee.

Most inshore fish take prawns, including wrasse, bass, pollack and flatties. Light float tackle is the most pleasing method. Stick a size 6 short shank hook in the prawn's tail so it can move naturally. Incidentally, prawns which are heavily laden with eggs produce more fish...but don't ask me why!

Prawns will only stay alive if they are kept in a bucket of seawater with a portable aerator. They quickly perish once left out of water. If you want to keep prawns for long periods the water temperature will need to be far higher than that for most other baits, approximately 55 degrees Fahrenheit. Regular changes of water are also necessary as bacteria multiply quickly in the warm water.

Slipper limpets

The slipper limpet has become a favourite winter bait with South Coast anglers. It is a relative newcomer to this country but is now found on many beaches south of the Wash and is spreading at a remarkable rate.

Unlike other shellfish, the slipper limpet gathers together in clusters with as many as a dozen stuck together. The largest ones on the bottom of the stack are always females and anchor the community to a stone. After a south-westerly gale, large

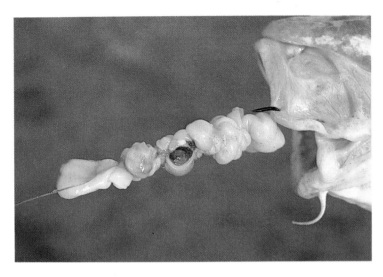

Razorfish lashed to the hook will turn any cod's head.

How to present a sandeel.

quantities of limpets get washed up on the high tide mark. Some estuaries hold a good stock and oyster fishermen regularly dredge them up.

Once the limpets have been prised apart, a soft, yellowish flesh is exposed which can be scooped out and used as bait. Although many species accept freshly collected limpets, catches will improve by using stale, smelly baits which are at least two weeks old. Storage is simply a matter of placing them in a damp hessian sack

in a cool corner out of direct sunlight.

It's a fiddling job removing limpets from their shell and I usually fill a jam jar with them at home before heading for the beach. Slide the handle of an old teaspoon under the fleshy part of the limpet and it will slip out of its shell. A Baitsafe is required with fresh limpets as they disintegrate on the lightest of casts. Older limpets are a great deal tougher and cause fewer problems.

Winter specials

Slipper limpets will catch fish for most of the year but I rate them indispensable in late winter when storms present the flatfish with a harvest of shellfish disturbed by turbulence. A size 2 Aberdeen crammed with six limpets takes fish after fish at these times. Although they are not recognised cod bait, limpets are frequently effective during December and January when they're capable of singling out heavyweights.

Freezing method

To freeze slipper limpets, shell some week-old ones and place the fleshy parts on absorbent paper to dry. After a couple of hours transfer them to a sheet of newspaper, sprinkle on some salt and leave overnight. Remove any surplus salt the following day before packaging the limpets in batches of 40 ready for the freezer.

Most shellfish salted and frozen in this manner will become significantly tougher than the natural bait and that adds up to problem-free casting.

Razorfish

The razorfish was once the most popular shellfish but the big freeze of 1963 killed off vast numbers and the species has not fully recovered. Fortunately, it appears to be making a comeback on south- and west-facing coasts.

There are four main varieties, ranging in size from 11cm to 20cm. The razorfish lives up to its name as the edge of the shell can be exceptionally sharp. They fish prefer a flat, sandy bottom where they can quickly bury themselves when danger threatens. They'll sometimes root down for several feet.

Although razorfish can be collected after a big storm in the same way as slipper limpets, they are also seen sticking out above the surface of the sand at the low-water mark during spring equinox tides. They must be approached stealthily because they disappear in an instant. And do not pull too vigorously because they anchor themselves in the sand with a toe and break easily.

On some beaches, razorfish will emerge at the surface if salt is sprinkled down their hole. It's thought this tricks them into believing that the tide has started to flood.

The razorfish is another delicate bait and like limpets they'll produce better results when they're a few days old. Most flatfish take razorfish along with bass, cod, eels and pouting. Like any other shellfish, the peak time to fish them is after storms. A size 2 Aberdeen hook is more than adequate.

They are an ideal bait to freeze. Just wrap them individually in newspaper and pop them in the freezer. To make them tougher, salt and freeze in the same manner as slipper limpet.

Other shellfish

There are several other shellfish, such as whelks, cockles, rock limpets and butterfish, which only seem to work on a regional basis. But the mussel is worthy of special mention. It clings in clumps to groynes and support structures of piers. Along the north-east coast it is highly rated for cod and flatties. Elsewhere, few anglers seem to give mussels serious consideration.

The mussel's soft, fleshy contents will not withstand casting in the natural state unless used on light float tackle. To harden up the mussel, it must be salted, like limpets, although freezing isn't necessary. Mussel becomes very tough once salted and serves as a superb cod bait. Hook choice varies depending on the type of fishing.

Sandeels

Sandeels are a premier bait for bass but many beach anglers shy away from using them because of the difficulties of collection and storage.

In spring and early summer, the arrival of sandeels is the signal for large predatory fish such as rays and bass to move within casting range. But plaice, dabs, pout, flounders and doggies also feed avidly on legered eels and float or spinning tackle accounts for garfish, mackerel, pollack and scad.

Fresh sandeels usually outfish frozen bait with the exception of doggies which dis-

Cutting up a Mackerel
Top left: Cut a fillet away from your body.

Top: Trap the fillet in position with a second, smaller hook on the snood.

Above left: Cut small strips as shown and then slide filleting knife along backbone to remove them all.

Above: Ragworm tipped with mackerel – a really juicy cocktail.

Whole squid is one of the best attractors for double-figure cod.

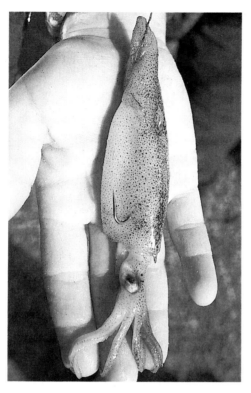

Freezing techniques

There's a method of freezing that allows sandeels to thaw out as good as new – but they must be kept alive right up to the last moment. First, rinse the eels in freshwater and dry individually. Then lay them out separately on newspaper. Deposit them in the coldest part of the freezer and, once frozen, package them as required.

Hooking methods

I like to fish sandeels in the tidal stream on a light spinning rod with a 1oz ball weight and 3ft flowing trace. For light line or float work, the hook is passed right through the head by the eye and then out again about half-an-inch further down just behind the gill cover. Make sure the point of the hook is not covered.

Presentation is not quite so important when bottom fishing for rays and doggies but I favour passing the wire hook directly through the eel's mouth, down through the body and emerging approximately 1.5in from the eel's tail. To prevent the eel being ripped off while beachcasting, whip it on securely with elastic thread.

Mackerel

This is one of the outstanding fish baits. It is a major food source for many larger sea species but Eastern Bloc factory-ships ripped a hole in its numbers through over-fishing in the Western Approaches.

Catching mackerel

The three main methods of catching mackerel are feathering, floatfishing and spinning. Feathering is the obvious choice if you want to catch them in numbers purely for bait. Mackerel shoals are easy to spot as they move inshore to chase small fry which boil on the surface in mad panic. Terns and gulls also hover just above the shoals to feed on any small fish breaking the surface.

Once a shoal has been sighted, it's just a case of heaving out a string of six feathers and working them back through the shoal with repeated, quick sweeps of the rod and a steady retrieve.

play no preferences. Few tackle shops have the facilities to keep live sandeels. If you can't collect your own buy some which have been blast-frozen as they're always of the highest quality.

Catching sandeels

For the angler living close to the coast, netting is the easiest way of catching sandeels in numbers but the outlay on equipment is not viable unless the costs are shared between friends.

The alternative method is to go out and dig for them. It's relatively easy under the right tidal and weather conditions. The most prolific sandeel spots are on sand-bars where large numbers can be dug on warm, muggy nights during a big spring low-tide.

As the tide recedes, many sandeels bury down in the sand for a couple of inches and the only equipment required is a fork and a bucket filled with sea water. A portable aerator is essential if you want to keep them alive. Fork over the top three or four inches of sand, moving backwards. All you will see of the eels as you fork them out is a flash of silver as they try to bury themselves again.

along the entire length of the backbone until all the fillets are removed. These will be the right size for tipping off or can be used as bait in their own right.

Pout bait prepared for conger with the backbone removed so the fillets flap enticingly.

Freezing mackerel

If you want to freeze mackerel they must be gutted immediately after capture. That's the only sure way to guarantee a firm bait. Rinse the fish in freshwater as soon as possible and when dry wrap them individually in clingfilm before storing in the coldest part of the freezer. After a couple of days pack the mackerel in a heavy grade plastic bag with as much air expelled as possible. The bags should be tied to make them airtight. Bait frozen in this way will last for some time.

Presenting mackerel

Most beach rods are capable of casting a good sized fillet sliced from one side of the mackerel. Remember to cut away from your body with the mackerel resting on a flat surface. Hook size depends on the size of the fillet but a 5/0 O'Shaughnessy is more than adequate.

qhe problem with these bulky fillets is that they slide down the shank on the cast and cover the point of the hook. This can be avoided by using a smaller, second hook like a size 2 Kamasan or something similar to trap the fillet in place. Slide this smaller hook down the snood until the bottom third of the hook rests over the top of the bait. Then twist the snood around the shank several times to secure the hook. Finally, set the Kamasan firmly in the top of the fillet and the bait will hold fast to it.

Worm baits tipped off with small strips of mackerel are a useful ploy. To prepare these small strips make a series of deep cuts approximately quarter-of-an-inch apart diagonally across the flank of the fish. Then slide the sharp filleting knife

Squid

Squid is one of the top attractors for double-figure cod in winter. Pollack, rays and conger also like a whole squid, and smaller species, such as whiting and dabs, take it in thin strips.

Frozen squid can be bought from most tackle shops in 5lb packs. Thaw out a box just sufficiently to break the squid apart into smaller packs for re-freezing. Grade the squid at the same time. Larger pieces which are too big for casting should be kept together for cutting into strips. Do not thaw out the squid completely because it quickly deteriorates. If the flesh turns a pinkish colour then you have got problems – the bait is starting to go off.

Whole squid are mounted in a similar way to mackerel on a 5/0 hook. Once again a small bait-holding hook needs securing on the snood to hold everything rigid.

There will be times with squid when fish snap at the head and trailing tentacles without taking the whole bait. Big pollack often feed in this way and the solution is to impale two sizeable hooks in the head of a squid with the rest of it removed. Small squid strips go down well when fished as a cocktail with lugworm.

Herring

The oily herring leaves a superb scent trail on the seabed and its applications are similar to those of the mackerel. It works well in small strips either as a single bait or for tipping off worms in winter.

There are several other fish offerings, like sprat and pout, which are basically used whole as big fish baits for conger, rays and bull huss. In the case of pouting, a good fillet from an 8in fish or the head and guts make cracking conger fare. A secondary, bait-holding hook is always required for these presentations.

LINE, WEIGHTS AND RIGS

Mono safeguards

Swinging a heavy lead sinker on the seashore is a potentially lethal exercise. Sensible precautions must be taken to avoid the nylon monofilament snapping during casting and possibly hurtling the weight out of control towards other anglers. Clearly, safety-first measures start with the choice of a suitable line. For general legering purposes there are three distinct and quite separate considerations.

First, there is the reel or main line which should be at least 10lb breaking strain as an absolute minimum. This is followed by a shock leader of 50lb nylon to absorb the stresses imposed by casting. The shock leader is not optional –you owe it to fellow anglers on the beach to think of their safety. Then comes the short length of main trace line on which the snoods or hook lengths are hung. For the trace I use 60lb Daiwa which is both strong and supple.

The trace is heavier than the casting leader to compensate for the weakening effect of knots used to assemble the terminal rig. Remember that every time you tie a knot in nylon it reduces the breaking strain.

Reel lines

Apart from breaking strain, the diameter of the line also has to be taken into account when selecting a main reel line. There are significant differences between manufacturers on this score, with the same line strengths in rival brands varying considerably in diameter. Anglers with a good casting technique will certainly benefit by using lines with a lower diameter as they'll achieve longer distances. But these lines tend to be fairly stiff and knot strength is not all it could be. For the average angler, the larger diameter lines provide more secure knots and smoother casts. Recommended reel lines include Maxima, Drennan Beachcast and Shakespeare Superjet.

Jumbo spools of line are the most economic buy.

Economic bulk spools

Bulk spools holding 600 yards or more are the most economic buy for reel lines and I carry stocks of 10lb, 12lb, 15lb, 18lb, 25lb and 30lb. Colour does not really matter although brown or fawn snood lengths appear to outperform traditional blue lines.

Shock leaders

A 50lb shock leader tied to the reel line permits a thinner reel line to be used without fear of cracking off while casting. When preparing to cast, the leader should be long enough to run from the terminal trace back to the reel with half-a-dozen turns on the spool.

The shock leader is tied to the main reel line with the standard leader knot comprising a uni-knot and half-hitch. For extra security, it can be strengthened by doubling the loose end of the reel line back through the half-hitch. Dependable brands for leaders are Drennan and Maxima.

Hook snoods

Inevitably, hook lengths take a hammering when they're repeatedly retrieved over rough bottoms and crunched by fish with sharp teeth. Supple rather than hard nylon is preferable for snoods as it will withstand abrasion far better. But it also needs to be strong enough to deal with a decent fish.

You'll hear conflicting opinions on the most suitable breaking strain for snoods but I reckon between 20lb and 25lb is fine for most beach work. This may seem rather hefty for a hook length but lighter snoods have a tendency to twist and kink, often spinning fish from the hook on a fast retrieve.

The actual length of the snood is dependent on tidal conditions and fish movement but you won't go far wrong if you follow my specific suggestions for the various rigs which follow later in this chapter. The brand of line I prefer for snoods is 26lb Sylcast.

Weights

Shore weights or sinkers are moulded from lead. Their principal task is to provide casting weight for the baited trace and then anchor it to the seabed.

Neat leader knot slides easily through the top eye of the rod.

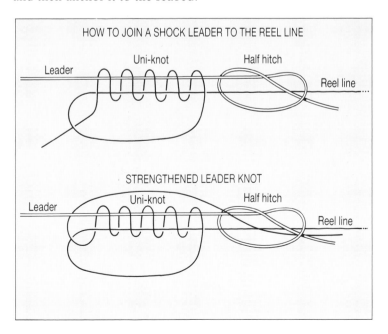

HOW TO JOIN A SHOCK LEADER TO THE REEL LINE

Leader — Uni-knot — Half hitch — Reel line

STRENGTHENED LEADER KNOT

Leader — Uni-knot — Half hitch — Reel line

Torpedo sinkers are the most aerodynamic and tumble along with the tide. The long-tailed version is more stable in flight.

The innovative Baitsafe protects fragile hookbaits like harbour rag within its hollow chamber during casting. Then the lid bursts open on hitting the water releasing the offering in perfect condition. Weights are added or deducted from the nose as needed.

Baitsafe

Plain torpedo leads

The profile of a sinker determines its casting efficiency and in this regard nothing compares with the aerodynamic shape of the torpedo lead. It offers minimum wind resistance as it cuts through the air, resulting in smoother, longer casts and more bait left intact on the hook.

Most leads are designed to grip the seabed but plain torpedo or bomb-shaped sinkers will tumble along with the tide covering a wide area and often producing

better catches than a static weight. This tactic works well at deep water marks like Chesil for plaice and dabs. The torpedo design is the one to use when shy feeding fish are deterred by the resistance of a grip lead with wires that dig into the seabed.

There are several other designs of weights in tackle shops such as the Bell, Pear and Pyramid but they're not as aerodynamic as the torpedo.

Long-tailed torpedo

The long-tailed torpedo has a 3-4in wire tail instead of the customary loop connector and it anchors the terminal tackle more effectively. It also stabilises the lead in flight and helps achieve greater control during the cast (see Chapter 5).

Breakaways

The popular Breakaway sinker with its collapsible grip wires is the weight for rough or windy conditions. The grippers

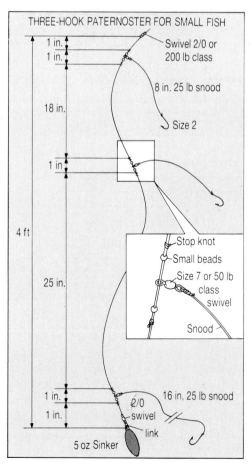

THREE-HOOK PATERNOSTER FOR SMALL FISH

- 1 in.
- 1 in.
- Swivel 2/0 or 200 lb class
- 8 in. 25 lb snood
- 18 in.
- Size 2
- 1 in.
- 4 ft
- Stop knot
- Small beads
- Size 7 or 50 lb class swivel
- Snood
- 25 in.
- 1 in.
- 1 in.
- 2/0 swivel
- 16 in. 25 lb snood
- link
- 5 oz Sinker

Grip lead for fast tides.

Latest versions of the Breakaway feature a more robust loop connector and trimmer beads.

hold fast in a moderate tide until you make a strike or a good fish takes the bait. Then the four wires spring clear of their fixed positions and swivel backwards out of the way so they do not impede the retrieve.

Breakaways often result in fish hooking themselves without any need to strike. Species like cod and pout are inclined to seize the bait with such force that they automatically pull the hook home against the firmly anchored Breakaway.

Long-tailed Breakaways are available for enhanced casting performance.

Fixed grip leads

These were widely used before the introduction of the Breakaway but nowadays they are only really called up when the strength of the tide makes it very difficult to hold bottom with any other sort of weight.

As their names suggests, fixed grip leads bite into the bottom at all times, even when retrieving. If a fixed grip won't hold then, it's a case of sitting it out until the pace of the tide subsides.

Flat weights

Flattened sinkers are the No.1 weight for rocky marks as they reduce tackle losses. Being flat, they act like an underwater kite on the retrieve, lifting the terminal

tackle to the surface in double quick time and missing many of the snags which would hang up a normal, conventional torpedo.

Unfortunately, they are not available commercially and must be made at home by using the two halves of a 6oz bomb mould (see Chapter 8).

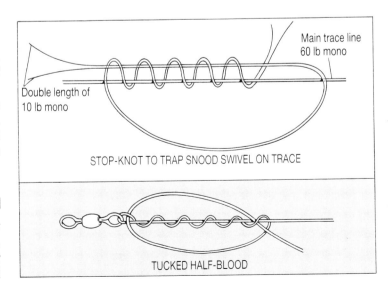

Double length of 10 lb mono

Main trace line 60 lb mono

STOP-KNOT TO TRAP SNOOD SWIVEL ON TRACE

TUCKED HALF-BLOOD

Flat lead planes to the surface faster over rocks.

Attaching sinkers to the trace

Never tie a heavy lead weight direct to the nylon trace because the knot will rapidly weaken when dragged over shingle and through pounding surf. It will even quickly deteriorate on flat, sandy beaches and after a couple of retrieves you'll run the risk of a crack-off.

The weight must hang from a robust connecting link such as a Mustad DC Easy-link, O-ring or a Berkley McMahon snap. Never use the American type snap links which can open up during the cast.

Sizes to carry

It's obvious that fast tide races or more turbulent seas will demand heavier sinkers to grip bottom than a sheltered estuary mark. But the strength and direction of the wind is another factor influencing sinker choice, while the amount of lead required to hold bottom can also vary at differing stages of the tide.

All rods have a minimum and maximum payload and the combined weight of the trace and sinker should never exceed the upper limit. The payload normally ranges between 4-8oz for most 12ft beachcasters. You'll find a range of sinkers between 3-6oz will cover most eventualities.

Swivels

Invest in stainless steel swivels made by top companies like Mustad and Berkley and quality is guaranteed. Brass swivels are a false economy because they quickly

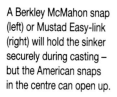

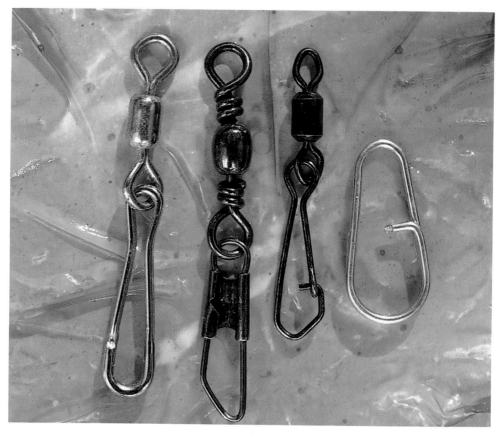

A Berkley McMahon snap (left) or Mustad Easy-link (right) will hold the sinker securely during casting – but the American snaps in the centre can open up.

corrode. The sizes are classified in much the same way as hooks, or in poundages to indicate the sort of loading they will tolerate. But there's no standardisation of sizes between brands and that causes a certain confusion! As a rough guide I use 2/0 or 200lb class swivels at the top and bottom of my terminal traces with No.7's (25lb) to hold the snoods.

Beads

There ares many uses for beads and they're an important component in many of my rigs. Haberdashery or art and craft shops are the best source for packets of small beads. Expect to pay around 50p for a packet of 500!

Terminal Rigs

Basic paternoster

Arguments always rage about the most efficient types of rigs but you can take it from me that the three-hook paternoster without frills reigns supreme. The hook snoods hang from the trace on swivels which are allowed a certain amount of free movement between stop-knots. It's the most tangle-free system yet devised.

Paternosters are usually made up with size 2 or 4 hooks to seek out flatties and other smaller species like pout, whiting, eels and rockling. But the rig will catch many other species of fish and if the chances of a heavyweight are high then I'd recommend the stronger Kamasan irons. But let's run through the construction to make matters abundantly clear.

Assembling basic paternoster

First, take 4ft of 60lb mono and tie a 2/0 swivel to one end using a tucked half-blood. This is more secure than the ortho-dox half-blood and is recommended for those parts of the trace exposed to maxi-mum stresses. Thread a small bead down the trace followed by a small, size 8 swivel and another bead. Repeat this operation twice more before tying another 2/0 swivel to the remaining loose end of the trace with a tucked half-blood.

Next, you need to trap groupings of two beads with a swivel in between at the positions on the trace indicated on page 37. The safest method is to tie stop knots on either side of the beads as these will not damage the trace. The beads allow the snoods to pivot more freely and act as

buffers to prevent the swivels rubbing against the stop knots. There should be approximately 1in of free play for the swivels and beads between the stop knots. It's customary to position the top two snoods close together with a longer snood on the bottom to drift in the tide flow.

Finally, tie the hook snoods to the three small swivels with tucked half-bloods. Again, follow the dimensions in the diagram making sure the snoods do not overlap one another. If this happens and a pair of hooks lock together the rig will get into an almighty tangle.

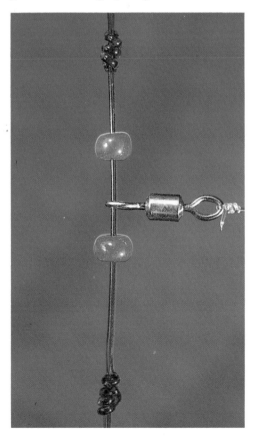

Let the snood swivel around the trace and the risk of fish spinning free on the retrieve is reduced.

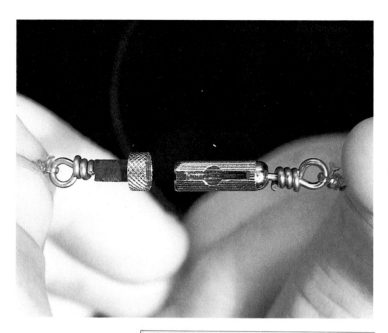

Aiken's quick-release clip saves a lot of time on the beach.

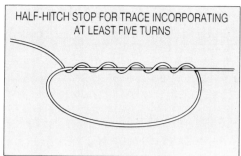

HALF-HITCH STOP FOR TRACE INCORPORATING AT LEAST FIVE TURNS

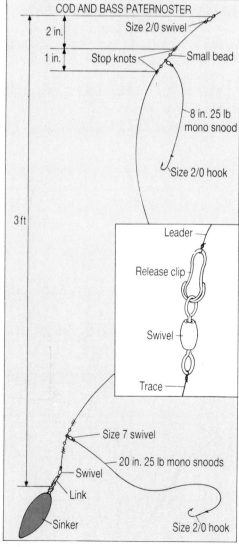

COD AND BASS PATERNOSTER

2 in. — Size 2/0 swivel
1 in. — Stop knots — Small bead

8 in. 25 lb mono snood

Size 2/0 hook

3 ft

Leader
Release clip
Swivel
Trace

Size 7 swivel
20 in. 25 lb mono snoods
Swivel
Link
Sinker
Size 2/0 hook

Cod and bass paternoster

As a starter rig for cod and bass, simply remove one of the snoods from the three-hook paternoster. Then you can use larger hooks like 2/0's and bigger baits without impairing casting distance.

Quick release clips

The casting leader can be tied direct to the 2/0 swivel at the top of the paternoster trace. Alternatively, use a quick-release clip like the McMahon snap, Aiken's spring-loaded model or the Mustad DC Easy-link. The quick-release clip is tied to the end of the casting leader and means you can maintain a ready-baited, spare paternoster in reserve to replace the one you've retrieved from the sea.

Using this quick-release system, it's amazing how much time is saved on the beach. The chief benefit is that you'll have a bait out in the water for much longer than if you had to reload all the hooks immediately after every retrieve.

Spacing snoods with half-hitches

Another method of making up the three-hook paternoster is with half-hitch stop knots tied in the trace itself. But there must be at least five turns in the knot. Anything less and the trace will constrict on itself and snap during the cast.

Assembly is much the same as before, starting with the initial 2/0 swivel. Then tie a half-hitch with five turns a couple of inches down the line and slide on the bead, small swivel and another bead. Position the second half-hitch within 1in or so if you can manage it. Repeat the sequence to achieve the correct spacing between snoods.

Ring the changes

Occasionally, fish may only take the top baits on a paternoster leaving the bottom one untouched. When that happens reposition the snood lengths so they all hang above the sinker. in windy or stormy conditions it's wise to cut the paternoster down to just two hooks to improve casting distance. These can be fixed above the lead or one above and one below.

Rough ground wrasse rig

A specialist rig is necessary to tackle the rock and kelp terrain preferred by wrasse. I eliminate as many swivels as possible and offer a simple set-up that is least likely to snag among the boulders. A heavy reel line of 30lb is fished straight through from reel to trace to help heave the tackle out of trouble. Most wrasse are caught within 40 yards of the shore making powerful casting unnecessary and this fact together with the hefty reel line makes it possible to dispense with the casting leader.

Constructing wrasse rig

A 3ft length of 60lb mono is the backbone of the trace. As some losses are inevitable in the tackle graveyard of wrasse country, you can tie one of the cheaper 2/0 brass swivels to one end. A stand-off loop is tied about 2in down the trace followed by a second stand-off a further 18in away. Attach a 2/0 brass swivel to the bottom of the trace and short 6in snoods of 20lb or 25lb mono to the stand-off loops. Give wrasse too much room for manoeuvre and they'll dive among the kelp in a flash.

Size 2 Mustad O'Shaughnessy hooks are the most suitable pattern but always have a small file handy to sharpen up the points because of the blunting effect of the rocks. Incidentally, the bottom hook on this rig should always be at least 6in above the sinker to avoid snags.

Rotten bottom

There are two ways of attaching the weight. If the seabed is particularly hostile then you'll need a length of weaker line linking the bottom trace swivel and sinker –a ruse known as a rotten bottom. Tie on around 8in of 25lb line and this lighter nylon will break first if the sinker becomes trapped, allowing the rest of the trace to be recovered. I tape around the top part of the weight and the first couple of inches up the line to give added protection over rough bottoms. It also saves using swivels and links on the sinker which are often lost to the depths.

Anything goes for weights over rough ground. You can make do with old spark plugs if necessary to avoid losing expensive lead sinkers. I normally use flat leads to plane the tackle to the surface and find losses are normally at acceptable levels.

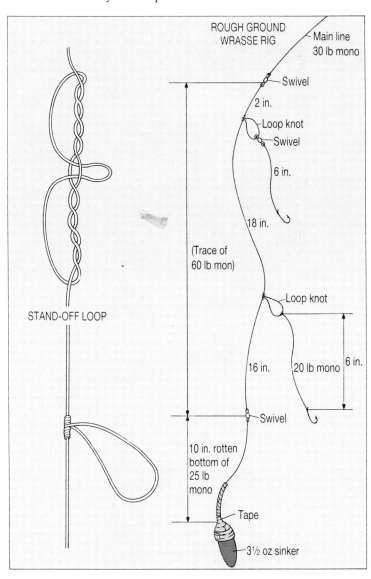

STAND-OFF LOOP

ROUGH GROUND WRASSE RIG — Main line 30 lb mono

Swivel

2 in.

Loop knot — Swivel

6 in.

18 in.

(Trace of 60 lb mon)

Loop knot

16 in.   20 lb mono   6 in.

Swivel

10 in. rotten bottom of 25 lb mono

Tape

3½ oz sinker

A crimping tool does a professional, safe job.

Wishbone rig

A long, flowing hook trace offers a bait more naturally in a moderate tidal flow than the relatively rigid paternoster presentations. in deep water cod fishing this often makes all the difference between success and failure. But the problem with long traces is that they severely curtail casting distance. The solution lies in the imaginatively named Wishbone rig.

These days I use a variation of the Wishbone called the See-Saw created by Portsmouth's Ian Golds. Its chief feature is a 4ft long snood which is held in place on the cast by a bait clip (see Chapter 5). A fixed grip or Breakaway sinker is a must and the Wishbone only truly works in a light to moderate tide. If the current is too strong and the sinker starts to move, the rig is liable to tangle.

Assembling wishbone rig

The basic rig is constructed on a 6ft length of 60lb mono. Thread two small beads and a small swivel, followed by the bait clip, onto the trace. Then tie 2/0 swivels to each end. Fix the two beads and swivel between

Lead-lifts

Instead of the rotten-bottom, a Lead-Lift can be incorporated in the trace when fishing a semi-rough seabed. This fin-shaped strip of plastic is about 2 1/2in long with a stainless steel wire running through its entire length with loops at both ends. The larger loop holds the weight and the smaller connects directly to the trace.

Surprisingly, Lead-Lifts have little effect on the cast and this is certainly the case with heavier lines. On the retrieve, water pressure on the side of this device forces it to the surface very quickly bringing the tackle clear of the bottom. Fish the Lead-Lift with a flat lead and you'll lose much less tackle.

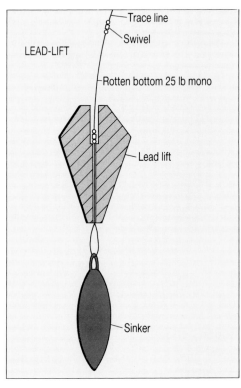

stop knots near the top of the trace (as shown on page 45) and then attach 4ft of 25lb mono to the small swivel. Another small swivel is tied to the other end of this loose snood. Thread a 20in length of 25lb line through the swivel on the bottom of the snood length. Then tie swivels to both ends of this line. Finally, tie two 6in hook lengths of 25lb line to both of these swivels followed by 2/0 hooks.

This trace is not as complicated as it sounds but it will take ten minutes to build! Both hooks are trapped against the bait clip during the cast and fall free once the rig hits the water.

A shorter version of the Wishbone rig is most effective for small fish.

Conger rigs

Conger are among the strongest and meanest fish found in our waters and there's the real possibility of meeting up with a 50-pounder. To take on this challenge, I normally make up a beefy fixed sinker rig which is similar to the paternoster although I only use one snood attached well down a 2ft trace. It's just the ticket

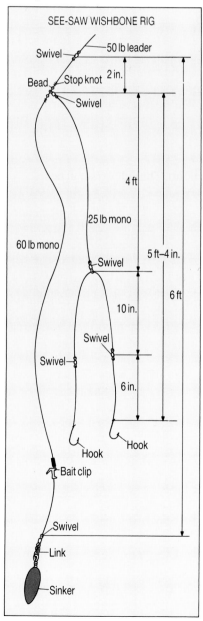

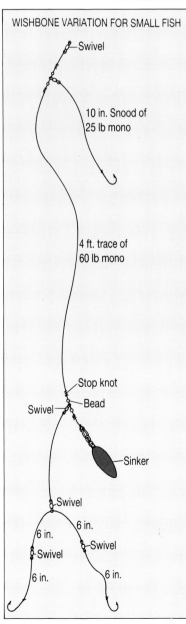

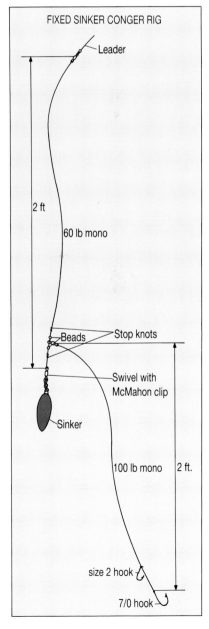

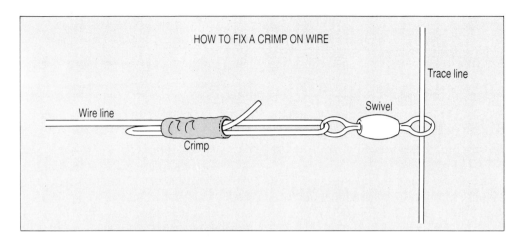

HOW TO FIX A CRIMP ON WIRE

Trace line

Wire line

Swivel

Crdit

Crimp

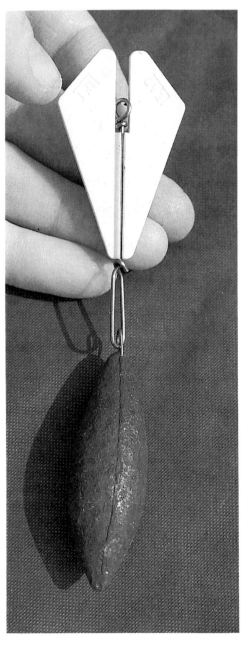

Lead-Lifts cast surprisingly well and certainly save on tackle.

for casting into a rough bottom where the conger must not be given even an inch of line. Big eels will soon wrap a muscular tail around a rock given half a chance or disappear down a bolt-hole. If that happens you could not budge them with a crane. Where the seabed is particularly intimidating a rotten bottom link to the weight is essential.

Constructing conger rig

My snood lengths are normally 2ft lengths of 100lb nylon. A pair of pliers are needed to tie knots in the darn stuff. Attacking it with scissors is useless! The beauty of heavy mono is that it will not twist or kink and is relatively cheap.

I occasionally use plastic coated wire which is widely advocated for conger because of their sharp teeth. But wire's tendency to kink over rough ground in the tide run can be fatal if you bend into a hefty eel. I only use wire with large, stainless steel swivels to minimise kinking at fairly clear marks where the tide is not severe.

Plastic coated wire leader is obtainable by the metre or in handy 25ft lengths on spools. I find 25-30lb breaking strain adequate. A purpose-made crimping tool is required to attach the wire to swivels and hooks. Never tie it direct without a crimp; it's asking for trouble. And unlike 100lb mono, pliers are non-starters because they're capable of cutting deep into the crimp and damaging the wire underneath.

For a professional looking crimp job, first thread the wire through a crimp, then

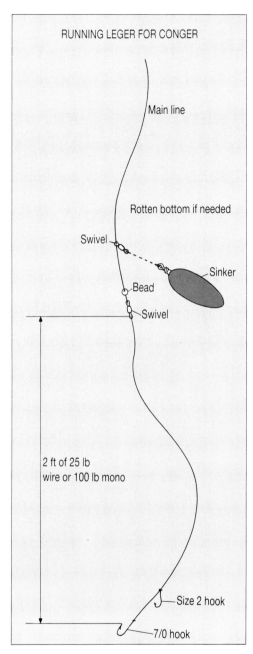

RUNNING LEGER FOR CONGER

Main line

Rotten bottom if needed

Swivel

Sinker

Bead

Swivel

2 ft of 25 lb
wire or 100 lb mono

Size 2 hook

7/0 hook

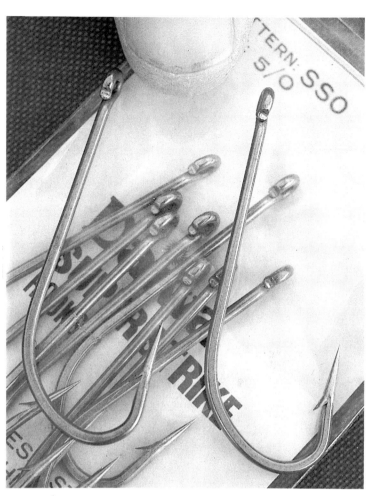

Running leger

Conger have a habit of playing with the bait and sometimes drop it when they feel the resistance of a fixed sinker. The answer is a running leger which shouldn't startle the fish as it allows the conger to take line unimpeded.

To construct this rig, first run a swivel on the main reel line followed by a bead and then tie the line directly to the trace swivel. The sinker is hung from the free running swivel on the main line with a clip or rotten bottom link. There are numerous links and booms on the market for constructing running legers but they cost a fortune and a solitary swivel does the job just as well at half the price.

Hooks and bait for conger are in the big league. I prefer the Daiwa Superstrike 5/0 or 7/0 stainless steel O'Shaughnessy pattern but also use a second bait-holder hook because of the size of the bait.

Conger hooks are in the big league and a packet like this should make up more than enough traces for the average trip. The beauty of stainless steel Superstrikes is that they can be resharpened.

through the eye of the hook or swivel and back again through the crimp. Double the wire through the crimp once more leaving a small length protruding at one side and a loop at the other. Now it's just a case of squeezing both ends of the crimp tight with the crimping tool. It's a most secure method which will accept a tremendous strain.

Store ready-prepared wire traces separately in envelopes or rig wallets. Coil the wire carefully and tape the loose ends to stop them unfolding.

RODS AND REELS

Underneath all the gleaming cosmetics of a beachcaster is the rod blank itself and it's the materials and method of construction that ultimately decide if this long, hollow, tapering tube will do what we expect of it. The blank must be powerful enough to hurl out a heavy lead in the teeth of a strong wind yet retain sufficient sensitivity to register the tiniest of bites.

The potentially tiring task of playing and beaching big fish in a heavy sea makes a lightweight construction preferable otherwise protesting muscles will destroy some of the pleasure!

The basic actions

Most mass produced beachcasters have an all-through action and flex throughout their length when under compression. They're only really suitable for simple layback styles of casting (see Chapter 5) as they would collapse under a full power pendulum.

But stiff or tip-actioned rods are designed as casting machines and react totally differently from a soft rod. The butt section is usually high quality carbon or aluminium to provide strength and rigidity. The matching top half is also stiff, apart from the tip section. Unlocking the latent power of a stiff blank can only be achieved by a competent pendulum caster.

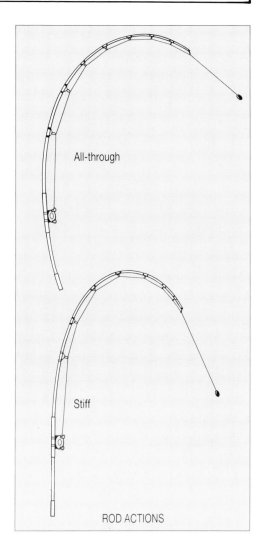

All-through

Stiff

ROD ACTIONS

Production rods clearly state the recommended casting weights.

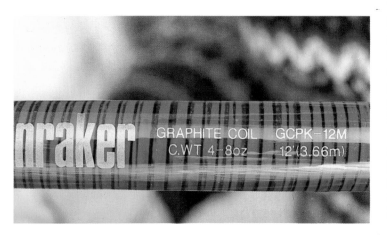

Recommended casting weights

Standard 12ft beachcasters usually accept a range of sinkers from 4oz upwards but they're frequently overloaded by anglers who forget to take the weight of the bait and terminal rig into account as well as the lead. Inevitably, that strips the rod of its true casting capability.

Rods with softer actions normally cast 4-6oz sinkers while stiffer models will take heavier leads up to 8oz. All production rods have the recommended casting weights clearly stamped just above the handle.

Choice of materials

Glass-fibre

There are still many budget-price rods on the market made of hollow, tubular glass-fibre designed to cast weights from 4oz. Glass gives excellent bite indication and the price of a 12ft rod starts as low as £30. But I've noticed some manufacturers are skimping on their budget series by turning out glass-fibre rods with wafer thin walls which could shatter while swinging a sinker. If you're thinking of buying one of these rods compare models on the racks and look particularly closely at the thickness of the glass wall around the spigot joints.

Glass-fibre beachcasters are normally made in two 6ft sections and have a soft, all-through action. But they're a dying breed now that the price of carbon has tumbled.

Carbon composites

Nearly all the popular mid-range beachcasters are loosely described as carbon but in many cases the actual material is a composite that includes a high percentage of other materials including glass. The amount of carbon in the blank may be quite small and the actions vary accordingly, depending on the percentage used.

Generally, the butt is appreciably stiffer than a glass rod but the top section might be extremely soft if the carbon content is low. A more rigid top points to a higher percentage of carbon in the blank.

A popular method of construction is to wrap a thin coil of graphite, either in an X-weave or coil, right around the outside of a carbon composite from butt to tip. This strengthens and stiffens the blank significantly.

Spend any time on the shoreline and you will soon realise that bass shine bright in the league of sporting fish.

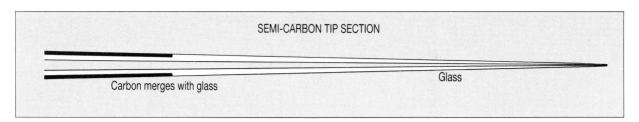

SEMI-CARBON TIP SECTION

Carbon merges with glass   Glass

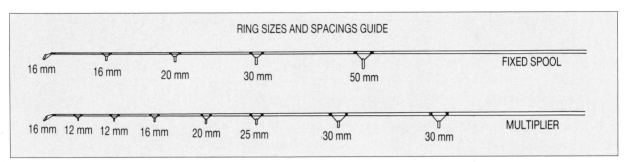

RING SIZES AND SPACINGS GUIDE

16 mm   16 mm   20 mm   30 mm   50 mm   FIXED SPOOL

16 mm 12 mm 12 mm 16 mm   20 mm 25 mm   30 mm   30 mm   MULTIPLIER

Semi-carbon

A marriage of separate carbon and glass sections in the same rod produces a versatile, high performance blank at a reasonable price that can cope with all styles of casting. The butt and lower part of the top section are carbon with the final 3ft or so of the tip made from glass-fibre.

These top of the range blanks are tailormade for pendulum casting and the glass-fibre tip shows up bites wonderfully well. The point where the two materials are spliced together is easily visible.

The top section of a semi-carbon is normally 8ft long with a shorter 4-5ft butt. Occasionally, plastic coated aluminium instead of carbon is used for the butt to reduce the cost of the rod. But this is likely to corrode as saltwater inevitably creeps under the plastic sheath.

Semi-carbon rods are widely available in blank form and many tackle shops offer a fitting-out service with the rings and reel seat of your choice. A limited range of ready-made models is also marketed but in truth there is nothing like having a semi-carbon finished to your own specifications – once you have gained the experience to know precisely what you want. All-carbon beachcasters are obtainable but at a price. The tips of these rods are rather brittle, in my view, and on balance I would say the semi-carbon is a better investment.

Rod rings

Whatever the type of beachcaster, it has to be fitted out with highly durable rings to resist the scouring effects of heavy line, saltwater and gritty sand particles. They should be as light as possible to avoid deadening the basic action of the blank. The more you pay for a rod the better class of ring you tend to get.

Types of ring

The choice rests between plain wire or hardened steel rings in a cushioned frame and models with aluminium oxide or silicone carbide inserts.

Plain wire rings are out because they're too frail for the beach and are easily crushed. But lined rings like the Fujis, which are justifiably popular in all sectors of fishing, have stood the test of time. Mind you, I'm wary of some cheaper lined models of uncertain origin as there's a tendency for the hardened inserts to spring clean out of the frame. If that happens to a tip ring then you're sunk. Suspect inserts have also been known to crack creating a sharp edge that could sever the fishing line.

Hard chromed steel and stainless rings reduce line friction to a minimum and add yards to the cast but the top eye is liable to become grooved through constant retrieving under pressure.

In my experience, the Daiwa Dynaflo rings are the pick of the pack and give years of trouble-free service. They have a very strong frame and low friction stainless steel insert which will soak up untold punishment.

Ring sizes

Line will only flow unhindered if the right-size rings are spaced out correctly along the blank. The number required depends on whether you use a multiplier reel or fixed spool.

Multipliers: rods fitted out for multipliers need seven rings plus a top eye to funnel the line smoothly. The largest 30mm diameter ring sits approximately 32in above the reel.

Although 12mm is the recommended size for the top eye I prefer one of 16mm. This provides more room for the leader knot to slip through on the retrieve, particularly if it is coated with weed. Admittedly, the larger eye slightly alters the rod's balance for casting but I am prepared to live with this knowing that there is little prospect of the leader knot jamming because of the odd scrap of flotsam carried up the line.

Fixed spool reels require a total of four larger intermediate rings plus the top eye to smooth the flow of line which whips on and off the face of the spool in large loops. Recommended diameter for the bottom ring fixed 40in above the reel is 50mm. Again, I like a 16mm top eye.

The awkward size of the bottom ring has been overcome by some manufacturers with a spring-loaded model which lies flat for transit and then clicks into position when needed.

Ring spacing

Mass produced beachcasters are not always spot-on with their ring spacing but it's generally good enough. The line must follow the natural curve of the rod without touching the blank or creating any sharp angles between the rings that could impose extra wear and destroy its performance.

If you intend having a blank made up then the correct spacing will be found by trial and error. The rings are temporarily taped in place and the rod flexed with a sinker suspended on the end of the line to check the positioning. Adjustments are made until the rings feed the line as parallel as possible to the curve of the blank.

Chris prefers a 16mm diameter tip ring (left) but most production rods are fitted with smaller eyes.

How to judge if the reel seat's in the right spot.

Screw-down coasters.

Whippings

Apart from being decorative and lashing the ring feet securely to the rod, whipping helps strengthen areas of stress near the spigot joints. Layers of varnish protect the whipping silk from disintegrating but for a totally waterproof seal hard resins are used.

Spigots

The most vulnerable spots on a beachcaster are the spigots which are inserted one inside the other to join the two halves of the rod. Male spigots reinforced with a solid centre rarely pose problems, but some female spigot walls are unbelievably thin and inadequately whipped. These are certain to crack or splinter completely in two when a pendulum caster winds up to a mighty chuck.

Thankfully, these shoddily made rods are in a minority and most come up to scratch with well-whipped spigots. Some rods even have a small stainless-steel band around the top of the female spigot for extra security. If you've got a rod with a thin female spigot, double up on the amount of whipping but avoid attempting power casting for obvious reasons.

Plastic coasters.

Reel seats

The screw-up Fuji FPS reel seat is in a class of its own and holds everything rock steady. Sand occasionally works under the thread and partly jams the screw lock but that's a minor irritation. Stainless steel reel seats with double locking collars seem more prone to gathering grit.

The majority of production rods fix the reel seat 2.5ft up from the butt cap which suits many anglers. But it means that others can't use the rod to its full potential. Pendulum casters often prefer the reel in a much lower position a few inches up from the butt and coasters give them this opportunity.

Coasters

Coasters are sophisticated Jubilee clips with screw-down, knurled knobs which are tightened to clamp the reel feet firmly

Locking Fuji reel seat.

to the rod. They're chiefly associated with custom-built beachcasters but a select few mass-produced models are also sold without a conventional reel seat so the angler can benefit from the flexibility of coasters.

The great advantage of coasters is that the reel can be positioned to suit your individual casting style. To find the right spot, tuck the rod butt under the arm and adjust the position of the reel until it's possible to rest a thumb or forefinger comfortably on the spool without bending or over-extending the arm.

Beware of sharp edges on the main clip of a coaster and rough corners on the knobs. These are the hallmarks of a poor design. Both these problems are overcome by plastic coasters.

Hand grips

Many top anglers dispense with bulky hand grips and leave the butt bare or at most cover it with shrink tube. That can make the rod slippery in the wet and uncomfortable to grasp in the cold. On balance, rubber Duplon type grips suit the majority.

Finally, a rubber or plastic bung should be pushed in the bottom of the butt section to protect the base of the blank from chipping on shingle.

Above: The bottom ring on a fixed spool rod needs to be large like this example of a quality pattern with hardened insert.

Left: Fold-down bottom ring.

Fixed spool reels versus multipliers

The choice in reels boils down to the simplicity of a fixed spool which is heavy and bulky or the more compact but exacting multiplier which transmits a greater feeling of direct contact with a fish.

Fixed spools have always been the first choice for novices because they are more tolerant of casting faults and you can learn to use one in minutes. But much greater control has to be exercised over a multiplier to avoid hideous birdsnests of line. The only certain way to live happily with a multiplier is to develop a smooth casting style...and that is asking a lot from a first-timer who is anxious to get fishing immediately.

Although a multiplier and fixed spool might have identical gear ratios, the latter recovers line much faster because of its larger spool. That's obviously helpful over snaggy ground where a speedy retrieve saves tackle losses.

But it's an open secret that most fixed spool reels were primarily developed for freshwater fishing. Manufacturers have simply increased the size of the components in the hope of satisfying the sea market. That is bound to perpetuate shortcomings and the multiplier is the reel of the future unless there is a major breakthrough in fixed spool development.

Above: Top of the range fixed spool with a reliable bail arm.

Right: This solidly built drag locks up tight for casting and that's the way it must be for safety reasons.

Fixed spools

An efficient bail arm roller is absolutely essential to guard against line wear and this is one department where the fixed spool makers have really got their act together. Smooth, hardened rollers which rotate under heavy loads protect the line at the critical pressure point and all modern fixed spools of quality now possess this important safety feature.

The bail arm itself should lock securely in the open position and not snap back if accidentally knocked. Bail arms which close prematurely are a positive menace. If it happens during casting then a crack-off is inevitable.

Spool size and line length

The average, large beachcasting reel has a spool diameter of at least 2.75in which will take approximately 400 yards of 15lb line. Nobody wants to go to the expense of using up that much main line.

To save costs it is usual to fill out the core of the spool with much heavier backing after attaching it with a timber hitch. Then the main line is loaded as evenly as possible until it is virtually flush with the outer rim of the spool.

This is necessary to ensure the line flows freely from the reel without scraping unduly against the lip of the spool. If the line emerges at an acute angle from deep within the spool, an enormous amount friction is created as it rubs around the rim

and casting is massively reduced.

Around 200 yards of main line should be ample on a fixed spool. There are times when an extra 100 yards on the spool is a necessity – for example, when fishing for speedy tope which cover 100 yards without stopping. But this is a very specialised exception and it's a fair bet that your first 50 yards on the spool will never see the light of day until it is replaced.

Line loading

To fill up with new line, slide a jumbo spool on a pencil and grip both sides, exerting slight pressure against both ends of the spool. Assuming you have got a helper to wind in, line can then be loaded under slight tension so that it beds down neatly on the reel spool with an even lay from top to bottom. Some fixed spools allow fine adjustments to be made to the line lay and that's a useful feature if the line bunches annoyingly at one point.

Drag systems

The slipping clutch or drag system on a fixed spool allows you to pre-set the spool tension so it releases line with the bail arm closed under pressure from a big fish. In theory, it absorbs any sudden, unexpected lunges that could snap the line.

Front drags: the most dependable system is a front drag which can be fully tightened down for casting and then loosened slightly to give line with the bail arm closed and the anti-reverse switch flicked on. Of course, if the anti-reverse is

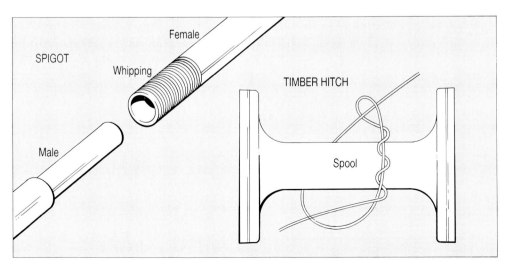

switched off when retrieving then it's possible to release line direct from the reel handle by back-winding. If you prefer that method then the front drag can be left locked up at all times.

The more compact multiplier gives a smoother performance.

Stern drags are now increasingly popular. They offer a more precise way of tuning in the required amount of tension, using a graduated scale which is clearly marked on the adjusting knob. But it's not always possible to fully tighten down the spool with stern-drag systems and that's potentially hazardous. Any slippage of the spool during casting could cause serious line burns and cuts to your forefinger even if it is protected (see Chapter 5).

Gear ratios

The gear ratio of a fixed spool reveals its operating speed. Depending on the size of the spool this determines how much line is recovered for every complete turn of the handle. A ratio of 3.8:1 is the average for large beachcasters and that retrieves slightly more than 15in of line for a single revolution of the handle. High-speed rates of retrieve are impractical for most types of beachfishing. Mechanics apart, there are enormous line twist problems involved.

Handle

Many fixed spools are ambidextrous which means the handle is detachable and can be screwed into either side of the reel for left-or right-hand wind. Handles must be large for beachcasting to ease the strain of reeling in through heavy seas and it helps if there's a good-sized grip knob.

Multipliers

These impressively engineered reels feed line directly from a revolving spool which is driven by gears on the retrieve. The spool is slipped into free running mode for casting and that is the moment when so many anglers get into a dreadful flap and find the multiplier such a handful.

Over-runs primarily develop with the free-running multiplier because of uncoordinated, jerky casting. You'll hear all kinds of theories about the causes but lack of control during casting is by far the most common fault. Line must flow continuously from a multiplier so the sinker speed through the air and spool revs are in

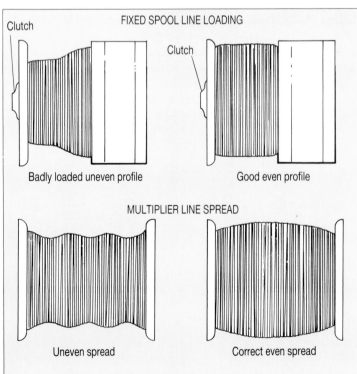

FIXED SPOOL LINE LOADING

Clutch

Clutch

Badly loaded uneven profile

Good even profile

MULTIPLIER LINE SPREAD

Uneven spread

Correct even spread

synchronisation. Once the spool revolves faster than the weight can haul the line, then it's tangle time.

The sinker splashdown also needs watching because it obviously leads to a dramatic reduction in speed while the multiplier is still zipping around. That is the moment to brake the multiplier manually with the thumb and avoid a snarl-up.

Spool speed

Multiplier spools accelerate from stationary to 40,000 revolutions a minute when a 5oz torpedo is cast 200 yards. And that happens within a tenth of a second! Any weaknesses in the bearings or elsewhere soon become apparent...not to mention any deficiencies on the part of the caster!

Line loading

Most multiplier reels for beachcasting hold around 300 yards of 15lb line. Backing is not normally needed. The mono must be distributed evenly across the width of the spool by the thumb or forefinger on the retrieve to maintain the reel's balance.

An evenly loaded spool greatly reduces the chance of a backlash by ensuring a free flow of line particularly at night or in windy conditions. The spool's capacity is also increased by an even spread of line.

Level-winds

A level-wind lays the line automatically between guide bars which feed from side to side across the spool while it is rotating on the retrieve.

Level-winds fitted on small reels take up a lot of room, making it difficult to get a good thumb-grip on the spool while casting which, in turn, cuts down on distance. The device also intrudes on line flow and if the leader knot snags between the narrow guides casting is again impaired.

Level-wind conversions

It's feasible to remove the level-wind mechanism from a small multiplier once you have mastered casting with this reel. Conversion kits are obtainable to remove the level-wind bars and internal gears. The top bar is also cut away and a solid crossbar fitted to strengthen the frame. Any screw holes left after the removal of the level-wind are filled with resin.

If you are not mechanically minded, then many tackle shops are prepared to do the work for a small charge. The chief reason for converting a reel is to gain extra casting distance. This can add up to a 20 per cent improvement on a small multiplier. Heavier lines can also be used as there are no guide bars to snag the knots.

Braking systems

At one time, multipliers relied totally on oil viscosity spread over the internal moving parts to slow the speed of the spool and it's still applied as a braking technique

A bulky leader knot is asking for trouble – it is sure to jam at a critical moment.

A level-wind guarantees perfect lay but at the expense of distance.

today. Thick oil is used in high summer when the normal grade becomes too runny and thin in the depths of winter.

But now there's a choice of more precise braking mechanisms including the latest magnetic models which the manufacturers claim can be adjusted to virtually eliminate over-runs.

Magnetic system: A series of magnets – usually eight – are fitted around the inside of the reel cage to generate a magnetic field which becomes stronger as the speed of the rotating spool increases. The effect of the magnetic forces on the aluminium spool is to progressively slow down its momentum.

An external dial with a graduated scale of click stops is adjusted to push the magnets closer towards the spool, increasing the power of the magnetic field and creating more braking power. Retracting the magnets decreases the field and allows the spool to revolve more freely.

The idea is that you dial in the required amount of magnetic braking to prevent over-runs and then gradually ease off as your casting proficiency with the multiplier improves. Experienced anglers remove the magnets completely so the spool is completely free-running.

Centrifugal system: the popular Daiwa Millionaire series, along with many other smaller multipliers, have a braking system that is governed by centrifugal force pushing a pair of brake blocks on the spool. The two, small hardened plastic blocks are fitted on spindles attached to one end of the spool. As the spool starts to rotate, centrifugal force pushes the blocks up the spindle against the stainless steel rim of the reel cage creating a braking effect. The faster the spool rotates, the more centrifugal force is set up and the greater the braking power.

Millionaire 6HM's form the backbone of my beachcasting. These have two brake blocks although I rarely find it necessary to use more than one. With a single block the line may start to fluff or lift slightly on the spool without actually birdsnesting. If this occurs the block is replaced with a larger one or I revert to the original pair. Multipliers can be controlled by tightening the bearing cap but I wouldn't recommend this method. I always set the cap so the spool is absolutely free running.

Star drag

A star drag or clutch is fitted to most multipliers just below the handle and operates in a similar manner to the fixed spool reel. It is tightened down for casting to prevent slippage.

Maintenance

Corrosion sets in faster than you think. After every trip to the beach make a habit of thoroughly washing your reel under the tap at home and dry it off with a towel. Reels benefit from an oiling once a month while multipliers will also need completely stripping down and cleaning about four times a year.

Multipliers fitted with magnetic braking systems are a good way of getting to grips with this type of reel – you simply dial in the strength of magnetism required to smooth out your casting faults.

The series of magnets fitted inside the Daiwa Magforce which help to progressively slow down the momentum of the spool.

Accessories

Rucksack

A large, heavy duty rucksack is much more convenient than a bulky tackle box. Many of the best fishing marks in my neck of the woods involve a considerable walk and a lightweight rucksack stuffed with tackle necessities makes the hike easier to contemplate.

Rod-stands

There are two principal designs: monopods and tripods. The metal or wooden monopod has a curved rest at the top to lean the rod against and a spike at the bottom for forcing into the sand.

On rocks or promenades you'll need the more versatile tripod. My favourite tripod is the Golds stand made from lightweight aluminium in 4ft 4in or 6ft versions. It has single and double rests to prop the rod against – they're interchangeable in seconds – and three separate positions for the

cups in which the rod butts sit. Other features include clips for suspending a bait bucket, and spare traces between the tripod legs and a welded foot rest at the bottom of the main shaft for pushing the stand into the sand if you want to use it as a monopod. Versatility indeed!

Umbrellas and brolly sheets

The protection of a 50in brolly makes life tolerable on the beach in wind and rain. You will need to wipe it down regularly to prolong its life. Corrosion on the shaft and spokes spreads like wildfire if it is packed away wet. Peg down the brolly firmly with a guy rope at all times on the exposed shoreline otherwise it will sail into orbit.

A brolly sheet shaped to fit round the back of the umbrella and clipped to either side stops rain and wind gusting under the umbrella canopy. Stones or sand are heaped along the back edge of the sheet to hold it down. Brolly sheets give a larger

Golds tripod is the most flexible rod stand in its class.

Rig wallets prevent traces tangling in the bottom of the tackle box. And if that's where you also store the filleting knife make sure it is sheathed.

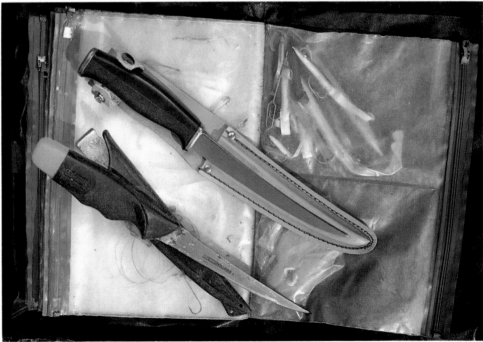

working area in the dry with more space to lay out tackle and bait in an orderly fashion.

Groundsheets

Over the years I have avoided losing countless small items in the sand or shingle by spreading out a large, heavy duty nylon groundsheet under the umbrella. Mine paid for itself in only a few months.

Gaff

I try to avoid using a gaff, apart from when fishing for conger and stingray, as it damages fish which might well warrant being returned. The gaff is simply a long pole with a large barbless hook lashed to one end. A small strap should be attached to the top of the handle for looping around your arm. It gives extra security when a large fish is doing its level best to wrest the gaff from your grasp.

If possible, it is best to gaff a conger under its bottom jaw and a stingray in the edge of the wing to give the fish a better chance of surviving. Never leave a gaff point unprotected; cover it with a cork.

Scissors

A pair of sharp, surgical scissors are the most versatile item in the tackle box. They'll cope with all the everyday tasks such as cutting leader line, trimming knots and baits and shelling shellfish. They are essential for removing the gills from peeler crabs.

Other jobs for scissors include cutting small strips of squid and fish bait for tipping off worms. Surgical scissors are the best buy as they will last for a couple of years.

Knifes

A sharp filleting knife is one of those purchases you take for granted but again it is worth spending that little bit more to obtain a quality product that will serve you well. Jobs for the knife include cutting up fish strips, filleting and gutting. Always use the knife on a flat, non-slip surface and cut away from your body to avoid accidents. When not in use, knives should always be stored in their protective sheath.

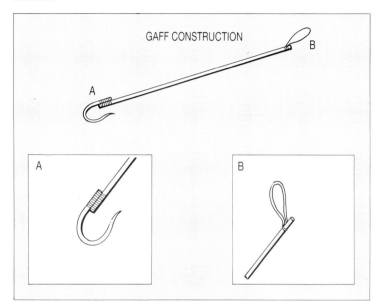

GAFF CONSTRUCTION

Rig wallets

A rig wallet contains a number of see-through plastic sleeves in which traces are stored in their own individual compartments. It is a tangle-free system that has been adopted by a good many anglers who previously kept their traces in containers like envelopes.

The wallets are sold in different sizes and hold upwards of 20 beach rigs.

Cantilever boxes

There are some really elaborate cantilever boxes on the market and the biggest of them will swallow an enormous amount of tackle. But one- or two-tray models are quite adequate to take essential items, such as swivels, beads, hook packets and spare spools of snood nylon, as well as all the other bits and pieces that you will acquire. Today's boxes are made from toughened plastics with durable hinges.

CASTING STYLES

Long distance casting looks impressive but in reality it's no guarantee of results. Regardless of whether a fish is feeding at 50 or 150 yards the key skill is a fluent casting technique which lands the bait on the seabed virtually intact. Poor, snatchy casts cause the bait to disintegrate in mid-air leaving little for the fish to chew on.

Safety

A 5oz torpedo reaches speeds of more than 100mph in the first 50 yards of a 200 yard cast. The potential consequences of a snap-off during this initial surge of acceleration are frightening to contemplate. A 50lb-class shock leader, strong stainless steel swivels and 60lb main trace are a must in the casting arena.

Grip for a fixed-spool

If your grip on the reel slips at the very moment when full power is applied to a cast, the distance will be much reduced and the sinker is liable to fly in any direction.

Before making a cast, tighten down the drag as tightly as possible until it's impossible to rotate the spool. The index finger

and thumb are then locked solidly around the rod just above the reel's stem leaving the forefinger free to trap the line. Release the bail arm and run the line over the forefinger which should be directly over or a fraction below the spool. If the finger grips the line above the spool, the mono will be ripped free before the cast is fully executed.

To guard against line burn and cuts, wear a finger-stall or the finger cut from an old rubber glove. There are several makes of line release-clips which trap the line instead of trusting the forefinger but I'm not in favour of them.

Finally, hold the bottom of the butt section with your free hand and you're now ready to cast.

How to grip a multiplier

Multipliers throw up a different set of problems with a rotating spool to control. The rod is grasped by all four fingers with the forefinger directly under the reel. If coasters are fitted then the forefinger is locked around the lower of the two clamps for extra grip. The thumb is placed on top of the spool, covering as much area as possible for a firm grip. Smaller multi-

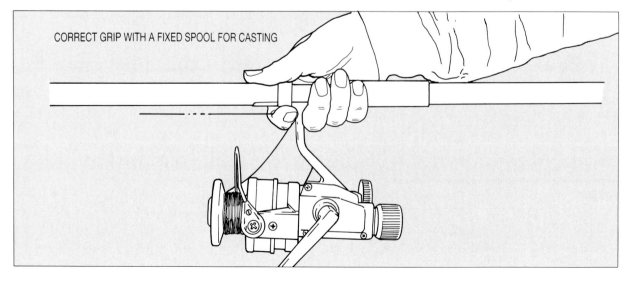

CORRECT GRIP WITH A FIXED SPOOL FOR CASTING

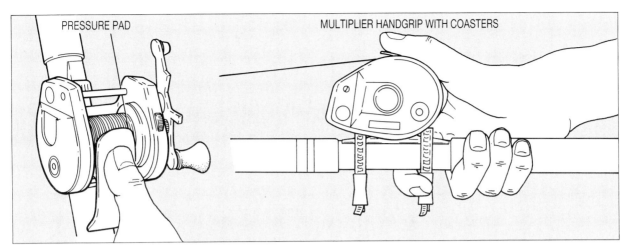

PRESSURE PAD

MULTIPLIER HANDGRIP WITH COASTERS

pliers with level-winds are more tricky to control as there's only a very small area of the spool available for thumbing. Full power should never be applied with these reels -you cannot exert enough downward pressure on the spool to hold it tight.

It's difficult to hold a multiplier spool rigid with the bare thumb when pendulum casting but a small rubber pressure pad helps considerably. This is normally a strip of rubber taped to the rod just below the reel. During casting it is forced down on the spool by the thumb until the moment of release. A rubber finger-stall can also be worn on the thumb to provide extra purchase.

Once you have a firm grip on the spool, release the free spool push-button and grasp the bottom of the butt section with your free hand.

Casting techniques

I describe four different casting styles on the following pages but to be honest there's nothing like man-to-man coaching to help build your confidence and competence. There are many qualified sea angling instructors throughout the country who are willing to run through the various techniques and iron out any faults.

The first three styles described –which meet the basic needs of most beach anglers when they are performed properly with mass production or soft-actioned rods –are the overhead thump, layback and off-the-ground casts. But remember that a 175 yard cast with a 5oz sinker is about the limit with a soft rod. For the fourth style, the pendulum, a stiff rod is essential.

Overhead thump

The overhead thump is the most basic form of casting and is much favoured by novices and youngsters. There are limitations on distance and bait presentation because of its snatchy action.

To start the cast, stand with the feet pointing at an angle to the sea as shown. With the butt in your left hand, raise your elbow to nose level pointing seawards. Lower the rod tip behind until the sinker, attached to a 5ft trace, just touches ground.

Once in position, turn and face towards the sea raising and punching the rod with your right arm while the left hand pulls the butt down and in towards the rib cage. At the same time the left knee should slightly bend, while the right leg is stretched and the body twisted to face towards the sea.

Follow the cast through with the rod tip pointing towards the sinker to cut down line friction. The exact timing of line release from the spool on the cast will soon become apparent after a couple of practise casts.

Lower rod tip
until sinker touches
ground raising left elbow
to nose level.

Follow through
with rod tip pointing
towards sinker.

OVERHEAD THUMP

Layback

The layback is a progression of the overhead thump with one significant difference – the sinker is moving before the actual cast is made, creating more compression in the rod and producing improved distances. The drop from rod tip to sinker is again around 5ft and a distance of 175 yards would be considered a very good layback cast.

The feet are virtually at right angles to the sea at the start. Twist and lean the body backwards as you go into the layback. The bottom of the butt is held just out from the groin while your other arm is partly outstretched and pointing the rod

Bottom of butt is held
just out from groin
and lead swing out
to right of rod tip.

Weight of sinker
bends rod into
curve as power
builds.

Rod held
high after release
with feet facing
out to sea.

LAYBACK

at a 40 degree angle from the beach.

The lead is swung up and backwards slightly out to the right of the rod tip. Once the sinker reaches the end of its swing you begin to pivot the body and feet to start pulling through the cast and putting the rod under compression.

The weight of the sinker bends the rod into a curve as the power builds up. As power still builds with the punching and lifting motion of the right arm and the pulling of the left, the rod's maximum height is achieved at which point the sinker is released.

The rod should again be held high after release to follow the lead's trajectory. This will slightly increase the casting distance. Your body and feet should now be facing out to sea with the right foot just in front of the left.

Above: Checking the drop at the start of the layback.

Left: A strip of rubber cut from an old car inner tube stops thumb burn with a multiplier.

Helicopter variation

There is a variation of the layback nicknamed the Helicopter which will certainly punch out long, smooth casts but the timing must be spot on.

The start of the cast is exactly the same as the layback but as the lead reaches the end of the outswing you bring it back

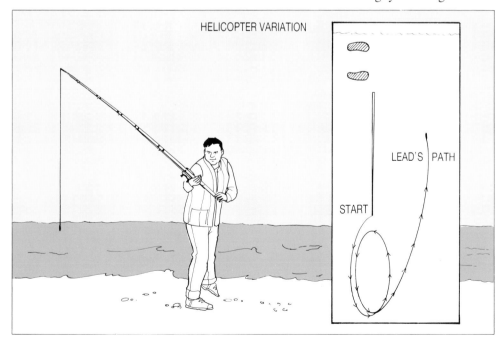

HELICOPTER VARIATION

LEAD'S PATH

START

towards you in an oval loop. As the sinker starts to return from the second outswing you increase the power and go into the cast in the normal manner. A well-timed cast will be very smooth resulting in excellent bait presentation. But get it wrong and the offering on your hook will explode.

Off-the-ground cast

The initial stance for this cast is completely different to the previous styles. The sinker is placed on the ground anywhere within an arc of between 180 and 270 degrees. The latter angle produces longer casts and is the one I will be describing here. The drop from the tip of the rod needs to be far longer, around 7ft being the norm.

Turning and facing 270 degrees to the sea, swing the sinker out so the trace is fully extended. This process is known as laying the line out. Leaving the trace on the ground, place your feet so that the right foot is pointing inland while the left is facing 90 degrees to the sea. At the same time your body should be pivoted and the rod tip lowered to within a few inches of the ground while keeping the trace line taut. The butt should now be just in front of your nose.

During this cast the sinker travels in an arc of 270 degrees, slowly getting higher. The main lifting and punching action

should start when the sinker is at 180 degrees to the sea. At this stage of the cast the power is considerably increased, putting the rod under full compression. Your body and feet also pivot as the cast progresses and you finish facing out to sea.

Follow through in the same manner as with the layback. This casting action is capable of achieving 200 yards.

Pendulum

The pendulum is the ultimate casting style and will zoom a 5oz sinker on its own well over 250 yards. But only stiff, purpose-built pendulum rods are suitable. Many softer rods will snap under the tremendous amount of power that is generated with a full-blooded pendulum.

At the start, the left foot should be at a 45 degree angle to the sea while the right is at about 135 degrees but slightly forward of the left foot. The body is now turned inland with the left hand grasping the butt around groin height while the right hand holds the reel slightly forward of the body at chest level. At this stage the sinker on the end of a 9ft drop should be at nose height.

The next phase is the outswing. This involves swinging the sinker inland at approximately 220 degrees. Once it has completed the outswing the weight automatically starts the inswing. The sinker

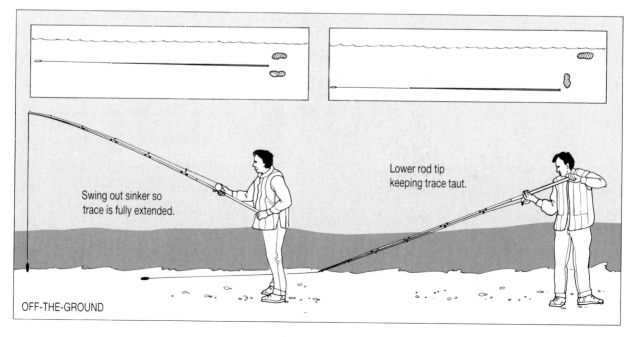

Swing out sinker so trace is fully extended.

Lower rod tip keeping trace taut.

OFF-THE-GROUND

flows back behind your head so that it is facing seawards. At the peak of this inswing the sinker stops momentarily. This is the critical stage of the cast. The moment you feel that sinker pause, the head is immediately turned seawards, the body starts to pivot and the blank begins to compress. As your body completely unwinds, most of your weight is transferred to the left foot. The left hand, which is now at nose height, starts to pull the butt of the rod down towards the rib cage.

While the left hand is pulling the rod down, the right arm is punching it forward generating maximum power. This has the effect of launching the sinker on an upwards flight path. At this stage your feet and body are facing directly out to sea. Follow the flight path of the sinker with the rod.

Casting faults

Poor timing and body movement and unbalanced foot placings all contribute to inefficient casting styles. Here are some other major faults which need special attention.

Loose clutch

An inadequately tightened clutch on a fixed-spool is certainly a cause for concern. The problem occurs when you start to build up the power of the cast. If the clutch is not completely locked and starts slipping, line will be released before you are ready, considerably reducing power and compression.

Pendulum Power
From left to right:

1. Ready for the off at the start of the outswing.

2. Inswing with the lead behind the head.

3. Midway through the cast and full compression starts to come in.

4. Watch for splashdown.

Finish the sequence facing out to sea.

Body and feet pivot as cast progresses.

BAIT CLIPS

Weak bail arm

The spring activated bail arm on fixed spools can occasionally snap shut prematurely during casting resulting in a crack-off. There is a simple remedy – discard the bail arm. It's an easy operation with most models. Unscrew and remove the arm from one side and cut it at the other end with a hacksaw. Leave the line roller in place for retrieving in the usual manner. Clearly, you will have to hook line on and off the roller manually.

Rather than resorting to a hacksaw, some anglers fix a small elasticated clip to the reel which connects to the bail arm in the open position. This prevents the bail arm closing.

Wrong drops

The drop is the distance between the rod tip and sinker. If if it's too short the rod will not be fully compressed during the cast. Alternatively, if the drop is too long compression will again be lost and the cast is likely to be wayward.

Stop knot
Bead

Turn-over period

The turn-over period only lasts for a split-second. As full power is applied on a pendulum cast, the sinker flips 180 degrees from facing nose-down at the back of the arc to nose-first as it is launched seawards.

Because the turn-over is so short it is important that the lead enters it smoothly, the final point of the inswing being the crucial phase. At the peak of this inswing the sinker momentarily comes to a stop and can sometimes wobble. If this happens it will completely destroy the cast's momentum and turn-over period. A long-tailed lead performs more smoothly at this critical stage and often turns a bad cast into a more acceptable effort.

Bait clips

The basic idea of bait clips is to streamline the tackle cutting down wind resistance and bait whiplash. As the rig hits the water, the line slackens releasing the baited hooks to tumble free on the sea-bed.

Never cram too much bait on the bend of a hook when using clips. I always try to leave the bend virtually bare where it rests on the clip. It's worth bearing in mind, incidentally, that a clip which is positioned close to the sinker rides in the slipstream of the weight and improves casting performance.

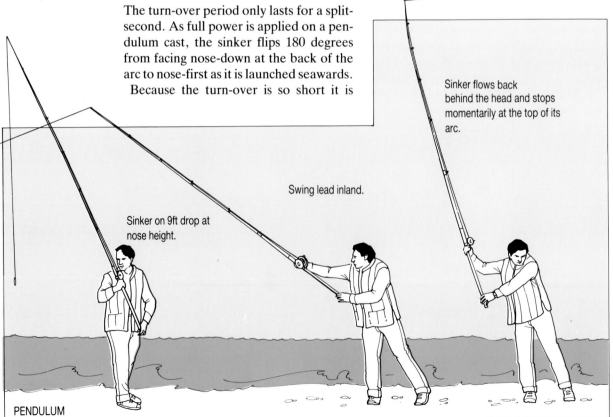

Sinker flows back behind the head and stops momentarily at the top of its arc.

Swing lead inland.

Sinker on 9ft drop at nose height.

PENDULUM

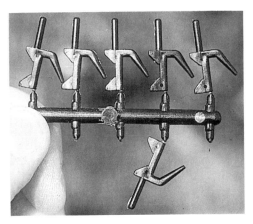

Far left: Plastic stops can
be bought in cheap kit
form.

Left: Simple bait clip
made from hook (left) and
purpose-made design.

Making your own clips

There are many commercially-made clips but they're easy to make for yourself. Take a long-shanked Aberdeen hook with a gape of around 5mm and snip off the point just above the barb with pliers. Thread the trace line through the eye of the hook and slide it up the line until it is in the approximate position where the hook will just reach. Then twist the trace around the hook shank several times to hold it in place.

Clipping up

Bait clips can be used for holding baited hooks up or down the line but care should be taken when clipping up. The pressure from a pendulum cast is likely to force the bait down the line well away from the hook, resulting in line bites. The solution is to tie a stop knot just above the bait to prevent it sliding. A small bead can also be pushed up to the stop knot for extra security.

The bait clips themselves also tend to slide on the main trace during casting and their position needs checking before each cast. Adjust them until the hook just reaches the clip again.

Reducers

Some top casters prefer the multiplier fixed right at the bottom of the butt. This allows them to flex the full length of the rod during the pendulum and gain extra yards. But it's an awkward position for the reel and a short 16in length of carbon known as a reducer is slipped into the butt to give the angler more control when retrieving. For the average angler they are not really practicable.

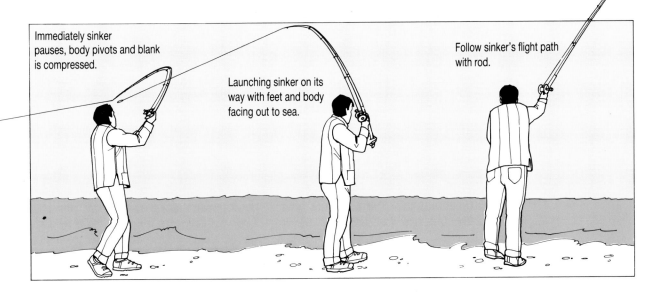

Immediately sinker pauses, body pivots and blank is compressed.

Launching sinker on its way with feet and body facing out to sea.

Follow sinker's flight path with rod.

ON THE BEACH

It's mid-July and the deep water lying off Dorset's Chesil beach is packed with its usual assortment of summer species. I'm confident of catching plaice, dabs, garfish and mackerel but if my luck's in there could be some hard fighting smoothhound as well. I make a couple of telephone calls to a Weymouth tackle shop and the secretary of the local club to check on the Chesil returns and both sources confirm there are plenty of fish within comfortable casting range.

Final preparations

Everything looks right but there are still questions outstanding. Firstly, will the weather and tides be favourable for my Sunday session? I must also make a judgement about the quantity of bait required. These decisions could make or break my day's sport before I set foot on the famous shingle Bank.

Weather forecast

I like to lay my plans for a pleasure trip at least a week in advance and pay particular attention to the long range weather forecast. Atmospheric conditions are the key feature. Low pressure is normally associated with wind and rain but in the days leading up to my session high pressure dominates the weather pattern.

Warm, sunny days and a light onshore breeze spell perfect conditions for flatties on Chesil which always produces a bumper crop of plaice and dabs when the water is gin-clear. The weather's on my side but what about the tides?

Big spring flood

It is pointless rolling up to the beach to find the sea ebbing away and with it your prospects of success. Consulting the tide tables takes minutes and it's time well spent. The tide for the coming Sunday looks excellent – a big Spring flood is expected to top out around 2pm. This means low water on my home patch further to the east will be during the early evening in midweek giving me the chance to dig fresh bait.

From past experience, the first five hours of the flood together with the first hour of the ebb normally yields most fish at Chesil. Taking all these factors into account I'll fish between 9am and 5pm on Sunday to take advantage of the most productive period.

Bait requirements

Now let's look at the bait requirements and calculate how much lugworm is likely to be chewed by the flatties. It will also pay to take some crab, with smoothhound in prospect, and as change baits I will pack ragworm and frozen sandeels.

The peeler and rag is best collected on Friday evening giving the worms 48 hours to harden on newspaper. As rag are a back-up bait, three dozen should see me through the session. I reckon two dozen peelers in prime moulting condition will serve for the smoothhound. Those crabs which are cracking around the base of the shell are held in the fridge until the morning to prevent them moulting too soon. Other crabs which are still fairly hard are left in a warm room and given a regular splash of saltwater to hasten the moult.

Lugworm blow in hot weather if they're dug too early and the safest time to collect them is the evening before the trip. In a typical six-hour session on Chesil I would normally get through 150 lug on just one rod with a two hook trace. It sounds a lot but assuming you make an average of six casts every hour with two worms per hook you'll need 144 worms to last out the full six hours.

Kit inspection

I always empty and repack my rucksack beforehand and refill the reels with fresh line after a couple of sessions. The 50lb shock leader is renewed after every trip. For Chesil I'll use my Millionaire 6HM multipliers loaded with 12lb and 15lb line and a small fixed spool to floatfish for garfish and mackerel.

·To hold bottom in the strong Chesil tide I'll take along 5oz long-tailed Breakaways together with a few 5oz plain torpedo weights for when the flow eases over high water. Then it's as well to examine the cantilever boxes to ensure there are sufficient swivels, beads, elasticated cotton and other smaller accessories.

With smoothhound in the vicinity I will probably make good use of size 3/0 Cox and Rawle Uptiders. But most of the time I'll be fishing with size 2 Kamasans. I am certain mackerel shoals will show at some stage during the session so I'll also pack some strings of feathers. Spare leader line, groundsheet, knives and rod-stand are all ticked off the list and that just leaves me with the rods to sort out.

It's not a tough decision. My 13ft Zziplex 2500M will handle the smoothhound and I'll set up a relatively light 12ft Daiwa High Performance beachcaster for the smaller species. A 10ft carp rod is packed in case I get the chance of some float-fishing.

Cool box

At first light on Sunday morning I load up the car. The forecast is for temperatures reaching the low 80's and I must take precautions to stop the bait cooking on the way. The rag and lug are placed in a cool box on a series of shelves with ice packs lining the bottom and I repeat the procedure for the crabs. The frozen sand-eels are in a Thermos flask which was left in the freezer overnight.

Where to fish?

With 18 miles of shingle making up the mighty Chesil Bank, choosing the correct spot appears daunting. West Bexington and Cogdon on the western limits are well known for producing quality bags of plaice but the beaches will be thronged with too many holidaymakers today. It's sure to be the same story of congestion at the Weymouth end of the Bank. That leaves me with Abbotsbury midway along Chesil, which I know is perfectly capable of churning out specimen fish.

But when I arrive at Abbotsbury car park there are already signs that holiday-makers are going to be out in force here as well. I decide to drive west along the narrow, bumpy track which runs parallel to the Bank and after a mile I've got the beach to myself. There are at least 100 yards of clear shingle without a holiday-

maker or another angler in sight. Absolute bliss. This area is unlikely to produce numbers of flatties but there is a real possibility of a hefty smoothhound or bass.

A brolly sheet makes a world of difference on a windy beach.

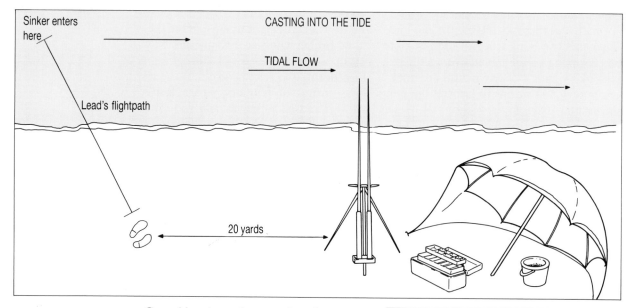

Sinker enters here

CASTING INTO THE TIDE

TIDAL FLOW

Lead's flightpath

20 yards

Crunching down the steep beach towards the water's edge I look for a patch of shingle that offers a flat casting platform just behind the high tide line. I also check there is no broken glass or other hazardous rubbish in the vicinity.

Rogue waves

Never lay out tackle too close to the low-water mark. Even on a flat sea there's the danger of a rogue wave crashing on the beach and swamping your gear. These unexpected waves are often caused by a passing container ship many miles out to sea or even a minor earth tremor. Today there's a fair swell pounding against the shingle and it makes good sense to stay well clear of potential trouble.

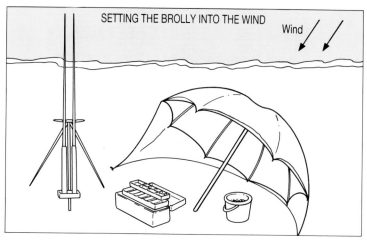

SETTING THE BROLLY INTO THE WIND

Wind

Setting up

First job is to set up the umbrella and brolly sheet to shield the bait from direct sunlight. A force 3 or 4 breeze often springs up by mid-afternoon on a hot summer's day so the brolly is set up facing directly into the wind. Before sorting out my tackle I lay the groundsheet underneath the brolly and the rod-stand is positioned where it can be seen at all times. The gaff with its point protected by a piece of cork is placed alongside.

Watch for splashdown

At this early stage of the tide there is a lot of flotsam surging past which indicates a fair tidal movement. I reckon smoothhound are likely to be out there and so I rig up the Zziplex 2500 with a Millionaire, 15lb main line and 50lb shock leader. I will start with a simple two hook paternoster trace.

The snoods are 18in long and carry the 3/0 Uptiders baited with whole peeler crabs tipped off with a couple of legs. Looking at the strong tide running from east to west it's obvious I will have to cast my 5oz Breakaway well uptide to allow the sinker to grip the seabed.

I move 20 yards along the beach before casting out about 100 yards at a 60 degree angle. I watch intently for the Breakaway to hit the water and then release line immediately so the lead sinks to the bottom as quickly as possible. If I had kept a tight line at the point of splashdown then the terminal tackle would have been swept downtide and towards the shore. A slack belly of line billowing in the tide assists in anchoring the Breakaway.

I walk back to the rod-stand, carefully tightening down to the lead and adjust the drag setting to release line under pressure from a big fish. The butt cups on the tripod are set at an intermediate level to keep the line up high and clear of the floating debris.

Types of bite

I barely had time to start making up a lighter rod for plaice and dabs when the Zziplex tip lurched over and a powerful fish made off with the crab bait in what looked like typical smoothhound fashion. Grabbing the rod I felt the fish lunging and struck firmly over my shoulder.

Chemically sharpened patterns penetrate very easily and excessive force on the strike can actually tear the hook from a fish's mouth. Allowance must be made for different species. Whiting and pout require a firm, quick strike but flounders must be given time to play around with the bait before actually swallowing it. They also seem to swim in pairs and delaying the strike will often result in both baits being taken.

Slack line bites are commonly experienced and they're dealt with by winding down quickly as the fish is heading straight for the beach. Once you feel the pressure of the fish, a firm strike should set the hook.

Strong running smoothie

There were no such complications with the fish hugging the bottom in the Chesil tidal flow. I was in direct contact and could feel its every twist and turn.

I always take my time while playing any size of fish. Fast, jerky retrieves can twist them clean off the hook. My recovery rate is slow and smooth and I let the fish take line when required. I do not favour the pumping action advocated by so many sea fishing pundits – you lose all sense of contact with a fast moving specimen. I keep the rod tip high in the early stages of the fight and as the fish is brought closer I realise by its size that it is indeed a smoothhound.

It sets off on several strong runs taking line from the reel. When it is about 20 yards away I walk into the edge of the surf to gain more control. It's going to be difficult beaching a fish of this size in today's swell and my timing must be spot on. If I catch it wrong just as the undertow of a wave is slurping back seawards, the fish will be torn from the hook. I wait until I see a big, surging swell. Then I lower the rod tip in anticipation, wind down on the fish and haul it towards me on the crest of the wave. I grab hold of the tail and dorsal fin and lift a fine 8lb starry smoothhound clear of the water.

Respect the catch

Smoothhounds, like other members of the dogfish family, need treating with respect. Their skin is like sandpaper and can rasp against your flesh drawing blood. I notice the hook is lodged firmly in the jaw making it easy to remove. After weighing and photographing it is slipped back into the surf. I'm against killing of any fish for no

Mackerel are worth their weight in silver to the food chain beneath the waves.

good reason. Most have tiny delicate scales which stick to dry hands and I would recommend using a damp cloth to hold your catch if it is not being retained for the table.

Tipped with sandeel

Catching a smoothie of that size on the first cast certainly gets the adrenalin flowing and I soon send another two crab baits screaming out seawards. Ten minutes or so elapse without another touch so I busy myself preparing the second rod with plaice and dabs in mind. This time the Millionaire is filled with 12lb line and a 5ft long flowing Wishbone rig with size 2 hooks. The bait on both hooks is lugworm but one is tipped off with a slither of sandeel. Long flowing traces always work well on Chesil, especially when the tide is pulling hard.

I punch the Wishbone rig uptide and with the hooks clipped down I achieve considerably more distance. My intention is to reach one of the many gullies that run parallel to the beach. The rod is placed in the double-headed stand next to the 2500M.

Different indications

A series of sharp raps on the rod tip suggests there are a lot of tiny pout and whiting in the gully. As a rule, these smaller fish tend to snatch at the bait giving a continuous indication on the rod.

Flounders and plaice suck in the worm producing a slow puckering motion while cod and smoothhound give a pronounced, very positive pull. This is more marked in a strong tide and the hook is often set as they pull against the fixed sinker. At other times you'll barely get any indication at all as the fish nose the bait and make no determined attempt to eat it.

Stirred into action

Suddenly I'm stirred into action by a harder knock and I reel in a small whiting

and a 12oz dab. The hooks are quickly removed and the fish returned before rebaiting and this time I drop the rig slightly closer inshore. No sooner had I placed the rod in the stand when the 2500M was again bending double under the strain of another hefty fish. A 10lb female smoothhound is responsible and it puts up a hectic struggle in the surf. That's two good smoothies in less than 30 minutes.

Meanwhile, the bites are coming thick and fast on the lighter rod from pout, whiting and poor cod. Among the stream of small fish is a dragonet with its dazzling colours. These fish have a sharp spine protruding from each side of the head which can inflict a nasty wound.

After a lull of 30 minutes it's time for a change of tactics. The lighter rod is rigged with a three-hook trace and a plain 5oz bomb in the hope that it will slowly drift around in the tide. The baits are also changed. Two of the small hooks are filled with ragworm and sandeel strip while the third is left loaded with lugworm.

Almost immediately the rod tip rattles as a fish plays with the bait, producing an unfamilar type of bite for Chesil. The culprit is a small silver eel which coils itself around the snood creating one heck of a tangle.

Fierce struggle

While I'm sorting out the slimy mess, the 2500M springs into life. The line falls slack as a fish grabs the bait and heads directly towards the beach. I take up the slack line until the fish nods its head. That's the sign to strike and I set the hook home. There's another fierce struggle and my second double-figure smoothhound of the session emerges through the white surf.

Then the plaice, dabs and whiting go on another feeding spree and after six hours of frantic sport I've recorded a splendid mixed bag of species. It's time to pack up and head for home after making sure I haven't left any litter. There hasn't even been time to think about setting up the float rod.

Keeping the catch fresh

Fish retained for the table should be killed by a blow to the back of the head and then gutted as soon as possible. In summer, the flesh deteriorates very quickly and the catch is best stored in a cool box with ice packs. In competitions where this is impractical, wrap the fish in damp cloths to prevent shrinkage.

Size-limits

Before any fish is retained, it must be measured to confirm it is above the minimum size-limits. The taking of any fish below the minimum lengths laid down by the Ministry is a serious offence. Spot checks are carried out by Ministry inspectors on both commercial and rod and line catches – nobody is excluded.

In general, it is probably wiser to observe the size-limits set by the National Federation of Sea Anglers which are above those set by the Ministry. There are regional variations in the Ministry size-limits which could trap the unwary. For example, the flounder limit in the Southern Sea Fisheries area is 10in compared with 9in in most other parts of the country. The aim of size-limits is to encourage conservation

Capture of a Smoothhound.

Left: Chris strides into the creamy Chesil surf to meet up with a smoothhound that's fought all the way to the drop-off.

Above: He waits for the right incoming wave and then uses it to help push the fish up the shingle.

Left: A quick march up the steep bank of peebles to unhook, weigh and then return a hard fighting autumn visitor.

giving immature fish the chance to reach breeding size before being scooped up by trawlers.

Measuring sticks

There are commercially-made measuring sticks but making your own is a simple task utilising a 16in long strip of aluminium with one end bent at a right angle as a stop. Mark out a scale in inches from 7in to 16in and this will cover most of the common species.

To measure a fish, lay it along the measuring stick and gently slide its head towards the end stop. If any part of the fish is touching the minimum mark for the species on your scale then it can be retained.

SPECIAL TECHNIQUES

Nightfishing

The popularity of nightfishing stems from the simple fact that it produces more fish than daytime sessions. The bigger specimens also tend to fall under the cover of darkness.

There is no great mystery about all this – it happens because many fish move out to the safety of deeper water during the day and are well out of reach of the most powerful of beachcasters. Others spend long periods buried in sand until darkness stirs them into moving inshore.

A minority of species feed exclusively by day. Wrasse are the most prominent of these – I have yet to catch one at night. Mackerel also feed mainly by sight during the daylight hours.

Nocturnal fish

As the smaller species head for the richer feeding grounds in the shallows at night they are followed by predators like rays, cod and conger. It is generally accepted that large conger in particular lie dormant by day, only leaving their rocky lairs in darkness. By contrast, small strap conger feed by day or night. Among the flatfish, soles are active nocturnal feeders.

But the most eagerly hunted species at night is cod. They're chiefly nocturnal feeders at inshore marks although when the water is highly coloured they feed just as avidly in the day. A good example of this is on the Durham beaches where coal dust is deposited and cod feed right around the clock in the murky waters. When the coal dust tipping was suspended

Flat calm on a summer's evening and the mullet are starting to move within casting range in the shallows.

You are never in the dark with a miner's headlight.

during the miners' strike the seas became clear and the Durham cod were suddenly impossible to catch in daylight. Point proved!

Night lights

Inevitably, nightfishing calls for specialised equipment including a reliable source of light to show up bites on the rod tip.

Torches

A small hand-held torch is a useful item to carry in the tackle bag as emergency back-up. But I would not recommend relying on a torch as a main source of light. They're expensive on batteries and it's impossible to play a fish with one hand while holding a torch in the other.

Paraffin lamps

Paraffin or petrol pressure lamps are the most widely used source of illumination on the beach at night. The amount of light generated is measured in candle power and output of different models varies from 200 to 500cp.

The principle behind these lamps is that a heated central tube vaporises the fuel.

As the gas escapes out through the fabric mantle at the top it ignites emitting an extremely bright light. The gauze mantle is very brittle and easily breaks if the lamp gets knocked about but it is surrounded by a glass bowl which helps keep out the elements.

Some of the more expensive models are fitted with a steel mesh on the outside of the bowl for added protection. An efficient pressure lamp generates a fair amount of heat which is comforting on cold winter evenings when the hands are half-frozen.

The big drawback with pressure lamps is that they are static and most times you will be forced to play fish in the pitch black. Paraffin also contaminates the hands and bait.

As a rule, these lamps should run for approximately eight hours on a single fill of fuel. The most popular makes on the market include the Tilley which has stood the test of time, the ever popular Anchor and the Petromex.

A lamp placed on the beach spreads light over a relatively limited area and is really only adequate for baiting up. A more effective pool of light is created by suspending the lamp from a stand. But it must not be allowed to swing in the wind – buy a stand with clamps that hold the lamp rock steady.

The light itself clips on the front of a toughened plastic safety helmet and the heavy battery pack is carried on a belt around the waist. It provides a powerful, narrow beam of light which is trained precisely where you want it at all times. A miner's lamp and power pack will set you back around £40 with another £30 for the special charger, but it will give years of trouble-free service and outlive any pressure lamp. Fully charged, the unit should provide 24 hours continuous light.

Two bulbs are fitted in the lamp and it's possible to switch between the two if the main one should fail. The weight of the battery and slight discomfort of the safety helmet are a small price to pay for absolute reliability and superior performance.

Isotopes

Isotopes are taped to the rod tip and glow brightly against the night sky showing up the slightest knock. The Betalight Tritium Isotope is again classified in candle power ratings and is supplied inside a protective, silicone-type tube. It is claimed the light source lasts up to six years if the isotope is not broken.

Reflective tape

A cheaper way of making the rod tip more visible is to bind the top 8in with reflective tape. Few production rods are supplied with this tape which is a pity because without it the rod tip just won't show up clearly enough against the night sky under the glow from a Tilley. The best source for this tape in a range of colours is a cycle shop.

Fluorescent tips glow after midnight as Chris watches intently for signs that the cod are about.

Headlights

Cheap plastic headlights fitted to headbands and powered by batteries are fine if used with a pressure lamp. But they are uneconomical as the sole source of light. The best system is the rechargeable miner's headlight. It's the most versatile, sturdy and dependable of all the night lights and ultimately the cheapest to run.

Casting at night

Distance casting is unnecessary at night because it's likely the fish will be feeding close inshore. As long as you have got a reasonably smooth casting style then night sessions should hold few terrors. Try to concentrate on your feet positions. If these are correct you'll have no difficulty casting accurately in the dark.

Floatfishing

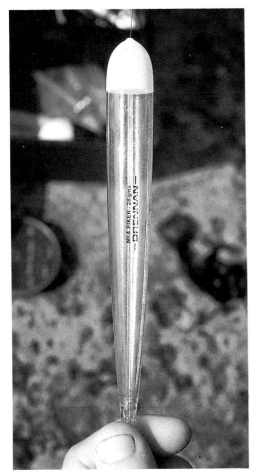

The potential effectiveness of a float rig is absurdly under-rated by most sea anglers who seem slaves to legering. In summer, many species move within casting distance of a float including sporting fighters like mackerel, garfish and mullet to say nothing of wrasse, coalfish and bass. Flounders can also be taken on float tackle in winter.

It goes without saying that the set-up needs to be rather heavier than rigs used in coarse fishing to cope with the swell and rough ground. A 1.75lb test curve carp rod and medium-sized fixed spool filled with 5lb to 8lb line achieves the right sort of balance. Cigar-shaped floats like the Drennan Piker No.4 ride the waves well in search of wrasse, pollack and mackerel while the lighter Avons with bulbous bodies are more suitable for flounders and shy mullet.

Streamlined slider float.

Flounder rig

First slide on a 4AAA Avon float before tying a small swivel to the end of the reel line. This prevents the flatties from spinning in the tide and twisting the line.

A jutting lower jaw and a sharp curve in the lateral line over the pectoral are the hallmarks of a pollack.

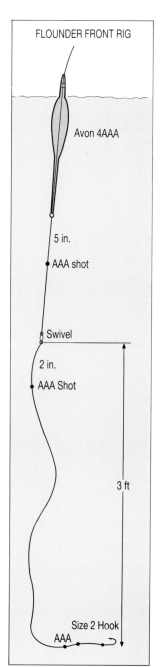

FLOUNDER FRONT RIG

Avon 4AAA

5 in.

AAA shot

Swivel

2 in.

AAA Shot

3 ft

Size 2 Hook

AAA

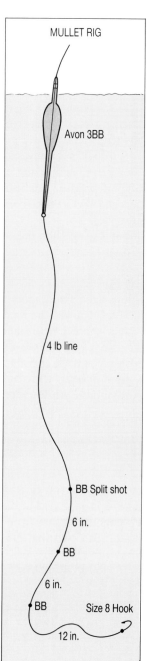

MULLET RIG

Avon 3BB

4 lb line

BB Split shot

6 in.

BB

6 in.

BB   Size 8 Hook

12 in.

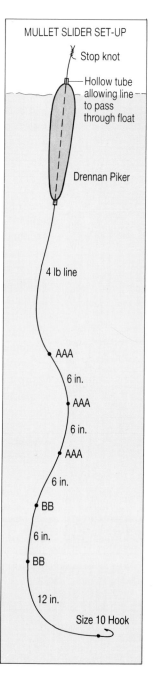

MULLET SLIDER SET-UP

Stop knot

Hollow tube allowing line to pass through float

Drennan Piker

4 lb line

AAA

6 in.

AAA

6 in.

AAA

6 in.

BB

6 in.

BB

12 in.

Size 10 Hook

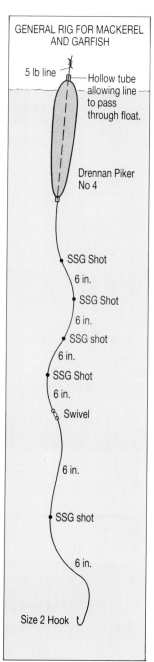

GENERAL RIG FOR MACKEREL AND GARFISH

5 lb line

Hollow tube allowing line to pass through float.

Drennan Piker No 4

SSG Shot

6 in.

SSG Shot

6 in.

SSG shot

6 in.

SSG Shot

6 in.

Swivel

6 in.

SSG shot

6 in.

Size 2 Hook

Attach a hook link of 5lb line to the swivel and tie on a size 2 or 4 fine wire Aberdeen. The float is set at just the right depth so the hook nudges bottom. That way it will stir up the mud as it drifts down on the tide and hopefully prove even more attractive to the inquisitive flounders.

My preferred shotting pattern to achieve this effect is shown in the diagram above. Please note the pair of shot fixed just above the hook which will help disturb the bottom mud.

Where to fish

A deep-water channel in a river estuary which runs near the shoreline is the sort of flattie mark which responds to a float if there's a fair run of tide. Just flick the float out a few yards and let it trundle along in the flow. A bite is often signalled by the float stopping dead but you should also strike at any sidewards movement. Flounders are not known for their fighting qualities but on light float tackle they're fair scrappers.

Mullet rig

The scaled down end rig for mullet reflects the shy biting reputation of this species. There is no need for a swivel while a size 8 or 10 hook is tied directly to the main line. The bottom shot should be at least 12in above the hook as indicated with the rest of the shot spaced out at intervals of 6in.

Sometimes mullet feed very deep down in the water alongside breakwaters and harbour walls and that is a job for the slider.

The smaller Drennan Pikers are handy for this task. A stop knot is tied at the correct depth and it should be adjusted during the session until you are able to find the correct level at which the fish are feeding.

Attracting mullet

Top baits are probably bread and maggots. To really attract mullet in numbers, hang a small mesh sack filled with bread that has been soaked in pilchard oil a couple of feet below the surface. Particles will filter out with the tide and maintain the mullets' interest.

Other rigs and landing net

For other species like mackerel and garfish follow the slider set-up on page 78 with a size 2 Daiwa or Mustad Aberdeen hook baited with a small sandeel or slither of mackerel.

The light lines used in floatfishing make it imperative to carry a landing net – the size depends on the extent of your ambitions!

A wrasse bites right at the rock edge and on light float tackle it's a sporting contest.

Impressive beak on a garfish – it's something of a surface acrobat.

Lure fishing

Mackerel feathers

These are normally sold in strings of six with a few, dyed chicken feathers whipped to the shank of each hook. The feathers are cast out with a sinker and retrieved by sweeping the rod back quickly, parallel to the shore, and then taking up the slack. This repeated pumping action incites mackerel into flinging themselves at the feathers in the mistaken belief that they are fleeing baitfish.

Many commercially-made feathers are tied to dangerously light traces of less than 50lb. With that in mind it is very prudent to avoid power-casting; just lob out the feathers instead, especially if fishing from a crowded beach or pier. The water around most groynes, piers and harbour walls hold a good stock of mackerel in summer.

Feather colours

The actual colour of the feathers is not that critical although on some days the mackerel might well show a preference.

Pollack certainly like white – mackerel might see red, yellow, green or blue as equally appetising.

Redgills

This rubber lure mimics the sandeel and on the retrieve its flexible tail flaps vigorously from side to side. It's truly deadly for pollack, bass and mackerel. Redgills really come into their own at rock marks where there's a fierce tide rip.

Use a long trace

A light 10ft spinning rod, fixed spool reel and 10lb line get the best from these lures and for weight I prefer a spiral lead. Tie up the rig as shown at the top of page 81 and use as long a trace between the swivel and Redgill as conditions allow – I fish a minimum of 4ft but on still days this is increased.

The Redgill is tied direct to the line by feeding the mono through the hollow nose section. The hook is then tied on and pulled back into the body cavity until the

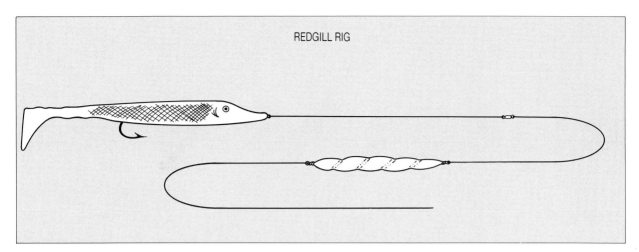

REDGILL RIG

just the bend and point are left protruding. Many hooks supplied with Redgills are far too big for beachfishing and should be replaced with a size 1 or 1/0.

The technique with a Redgill is to flick it out 20 yards or so into the tide race, pause until it sinks to midwater or just below and then start a slow, smooth retrieve. If you locate a large shoal of pollack or mackerel sport is sure to be hectic.

Spoons

The choice in spoons lies between plain white plastic and stainless steel. Frankly, there's no contest – the steel or flounder spoons are much superior in my book and produce outstanding catches from muddy estuaries.

The dish-shaped spoon is fitted with two small swivels at one end. The main reel line is tied to one of the swivels and a short length of mono with a size 2 Aberdeen hook attached dangles from the other. This short snood is usually 6in long.

Spoons can be fished on a beachcaster and 5oz sinker but the fight will be rather one-sided. Far better to tackle up with a light spinning rod, fixed spool reel and 10lb line with a 1oz weight stopped about 10in away from the spoon by a small swivel.

Spoon technique

As a flounder spoon is slowly retrieved it flickers and wobbles from side to side stirring up the bottom. Flounders will follow in its wake and often take the baited hook trailing a few inches behind. This method is most effective in the summer months when crabs can demolish static baits in seconds. A slowly moving spoon beats the bait robbers.

Plugs and Rapalas

These lures are realistic imitators of baitfish and many are fitted with a flexible vane, the angle of which can be adjusted to fish at varying depths.

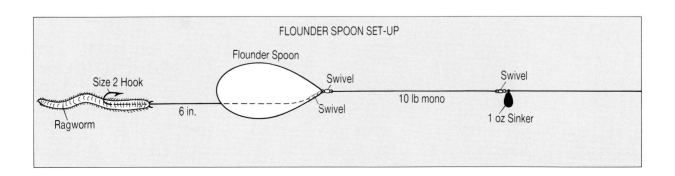

FLOUNDER SPOON SET-UP

Flounder Spoon

Size 2 Hook

Swivel

Swivel

Swivel

10 lb mono

Ragworm

6 in.

Swivel

1 oz Sinker

Spoon, Rapala or spinner
– they are all equally
effective on their day.

There is such a massive range of plugs on the market with a range of actions from deep divers to surface skimmers that it's tough to sort out the most killing patterns. But the Rebel J30S stands out for tricking the big bass.

Rapalas are essentially shallow working lures which float at rest and for that reason they are extremely well suited to snaggy ground –just the sort of territory in which you are most likely to find hefty sea bass.

Spinners

A small Mepps No.1 or 2 spinner will tease difficult harbour mullet into making a wrong move, particularly if the treble hook is tipped off with ragworm. The tackle needs to be as light as possible to avoid using a sinker.

Mullet, garfish, pollack and even small whiting snap at these small lures with gusto.

Pier fishing

The rusting metal of the support structures of piers with their covering of mussels, barnacles and seaweed present rich pickings for a multitude of fish in what otherwise might be a relatively barren area of seabed.

The bottom below piers is strewn with debris attracting colonies of crabs, winkles, cockles, shrimps and other crustaceans. It all adds up to the perfect refuge for many larger predators along with multitudes of smaller fodder fish.

Dancing Ledge in the Dorset Purbecks where the rock fishing is superb for bass, wrasse and conger.

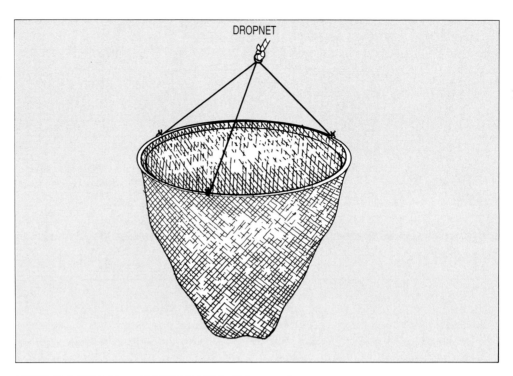

Casting from a pier

The outer stems of many piers extend over deep water and with the fish almost certainly shoaled underneath your feet there is no reason to indulge in strenuous casting. Never attempt a power cast on the pier because of the danger to other anglers and the public. Stick with a straight overhead thump which is relatively safe.

Pier tackle

Tackling up for pier fishing really demands a shorter beachcaster of 11ft. This gives more control over a fish that's some way below your feet. Terminal tackle is similar to that in beachfishing but obviously there's no bait clips on the trace.

If you are casting out about 30 yards and letting the rig settle on the seabed then the snood lengths are identical to those used on the beach. But if you intend to simply drop the baited trace down the side of the pier, use a longer bottom snood so it rests on the seabed. The other snoods further up the trace should be fairly short – about 4in is fine. Once the sinker touches bottom do not release any more line otherwise it will all lie in a heap. Keep everything as taut as possible.

If scad or pollack are about then consider rigging up with long booms on the trace and snoods of 10in These are fished well off the bottom and flutter in the tide.

Legering with a lightweight rod, single hook and rolling 1oz ball weight also offers exciting possibilities.

Using a dropnet

Obviously, it is risky hauling up a decent fish on the deck of a pier without the help of a dropnet. These are simple to construct using an old bicycle wheel with the spokes removed as the frame. Lash netting over the frame so that there is at least a 2ft belly in the mesh to take the weight of a fish. Three short lengths of rope spaced equally apart are tied to the rim with a steel ring link as indicated.

Drop a weight in the centre of the net, attach a suitable length of rope to the ring and lower away until the dropnet is about 18in below the surface. Guide your fish over the net and heave on the rope as quickly as possible to secure the catch.

Rock fishing

Fishing from rocks is exhilarating, challenging – and highly dangerous. It's easy to loose your foothold and topple into deep gullies and no fish on this planet is worth serious injury or death. Rogue waves which sweep up the rock face are probably the greatest hazard and many anglers have been swept out to sea from vantage points they considered completely safe.

Safety precautions

A hard safety helmet gives some protection against falling rocks and it's also wise to tackle rock fishing in pairs just in case of an emergency. Make sure you tell somebody where you are going and the time by which you expect to return.

Rock technique

In summer, huge shoals of mullet frequently move into quiet rocky coves to feed on maggots washed out from decaying weed on the beach by Spring tides. This presents the opportunity to take along a fly rod, floating line and a pint of succulent white maggots. Superglue a small piece of balsa to a size 8 hook to make it float and you can cast the maggots right on the mullet's nose.

Black bream are grand fighters given half a chance.

TACKLE CARE

Spend a few minutes each week checking over your kit and the effort will be repaid many times over. Corrosion bites amazingly quickly and if left unchecked will spread into every nook and cranny. A thorough wash-down of the outfit in tap water after every trip helps keep it at bay. But it's not just rods and reels that are at risk: swivels, line, hooks and sinkers are all subject to punishment.

Rod maintenance

Store rods in cloth bags to avoid unnecessary chips and scratches. Always give them a good rub down with a dry cloth after returning home. Pay special attention to rings and whippings which are very prone to corrosion. Grooved or cracked rings must be replaced at once. Whippings need renewing at the first hint of fraying. Brush any specks of sand and grit from the screw-up reel fitting.

Reel care

Reels are at most risk and require regular lubrication and maintenance.

Basic cleaning

The basic cleaning procedure is similar for fixed spools and multipliers. Wash them in freshwater after every trip and scrub out inaccessible corners with an old toothbrush. After rinsing, give them a rub down with a dry cloth and leave to dry in a warm room.

Lubricating multipliers

Multipliers, with their revolving spool, will need frequent dismantling and lubrication. Follow the manufacturer's instructions to the letter and lay out the parts in an orderly fashion. This makes reassembly far easier. Never use brute force to

slacken screws on the sideplates – if they're tight try some easing oil.

Regular servicing

A heavily used reel benefits from a monthly service and I adopt the following procedure with my Millionaires.

First, the screws holding the frame together are removed to release the spool. As the spool is eased from the cage, I keep an eye on the two small plastic brake blocks fitted on spindles which have a habit of getting lost if you are not careful.

Then the handle and star drag assembly is removed before slackening the sideplate screws to reveal the main working parts of the reel. Again, there's a danger of losing important components – the two pinion yoke springs. Watch them to make sure they don't jump out and get lost.

One of the best cleaning agents for removing grime and sludge is WD40. Use the long, straw-like nozzle to penetrate all the awkward corners. Once the reel is completely clean, rub it over with a dry cloth before lubricating and reassembling.

Repair or replace

However well you look after a reel there is bound to be grime and dirty oil around the main drive gears. Look for any tiny fragments of brass floating in the oil. This is a sure sign the pinion gear is reaching the end of its life. Other parts that show signs of wear should be replaced including fibre washers.

Weak spots on any multiplier are the rivets holding the reel foot to the main frame. If you are not careful, corrosion will eventually eat away at the studs until the whole foot breaks away from the cage. If this happens, don't consign the reel to the dustbin – the repair job is relatively straightforward.

First, drill out the old, broken studs and rub down the whole area with a brass wire brush rather than a steel one which is too

harsh. Then wash the reel in freshwater and dry it off. Spread a coating of Araldite to the frame where the two pieces join together before pop-rivetting the foot back to the frame again. It may prove necessary to file a fraction off the top of the rivets if they protrude and foul the rotating spool.

Maintenance is tedious but will lengthen your reel's life, improve performance and ultimately help put more fish on the beach.

Servicing departments

Many tackle shops undertake the servicing of reels if you do not fancy the job yourself or they can be sent back to the manufacturer. Here's a checklist of the major reel manufacturers offering back-up service.

Abu, Cross St, Lincoln.

Daiwa, Netherton Industrial Estate, Wishaw, Lanarkshire.

Leeda, 14 Cannon St, Southampton, Hants.

Penn Servicing, 33, Farleigh Rd, Pershore, Worcs.

Ryobi Masterline, Cotteswold Rd, Tewkesbury, Gloucs.

Shakespeare, PO Box 1, Broad Ground Rd, Lakeside, Redditch, Worcs.

Shimano, Unit B2, Phoenix Way, Swansea Enterprise Park, Llansamlet, Swansea, Glamorgan.

Other checks to make

Line

As stressed in earlier chapters, the shock leader should be renewed every time you go to the beach. Also, snip off the first five yards of main line which is sure to be abraded somewhere along its length.

The main line needs changing at regular intervals although the actual frequency

A beautifully marked plaice taken on crab from Chesil.

depends on seabed conditions. On sandy beaches, four sessions with the same line is fine but rocky marks may need the spool refilling after every trip. Do not store bulk spools of mono in direct sunlight otherwise they'll deteriorate.

Hooks

Chemically sharpened hooks should only be used for one outing before being replaced by new ones from your box. The heavy duty, stainless steel patterns can be washed and dried after use and resharpened on a stone ready for the next session.

Sinkers

Sinkers suffer even on flat, sandy beaches and if there's any sign of damage to the loop connector the weight should be discarded. From time to time, you'll recover a lost set of terminal tackle including the sinker which may have been rolling around the seabed for several months. Under no circumstances should these leads be used for casting. The connector loops are often made of brass which quickly weakens if left in saltwater for any length of time.

Odds and ends

The extending pole of a brolly soon seizes if it is not greased and the same applies to the screw-on metal heads of gaffs and landing nets. Pressure lamps should be rubbed down with a dry cloth and the jets also need cleaning from time to time. It's surprising how quickly they get furred up.

Tips

Moulding your own

There are excellent sinkers in the shops in virtually every size and shape you'll ever require but savings are possible if you have got the time and inclination to mould your own.

Safety precautions

Safety measures must be observed at all times if you are contemplating moulding your own lead weights. It should never be attempted by youngsters – molten lead can cause horrifying injuries. Protective goggles and heavy, gauntlet gloves are essential. Thick clothing and a hard hat are also advisable. Molten lead and water do not mix...it can spark a mini-explosion sending red-hot lead everywhere.

Method

My lead-making system is as follows. First, I cut the scrap lead for melting down into strips, removing scale and other debris, before placing it into the melting pot on a large gas burner. Normally, enough lead is put in the pot to produce a dozen 5oz weights.

As the lead is left to melt, the moulds – which are in two halves – are preheated with a blow lamp. Molten lead poured into cold moulds will harden before the empty chamber is completely filled.

I always use stainless-steel wire for the loop, cutting a length which will run virtually the whole length of the mould. This stops the loop getting pulled out by the force of a cast. I also turn the ends of the loop over at an angle to give added anchorage.

Once the lead has melted, any surface scum is removed by a large spoon and then it is poured into the mould which is held in a vice. After a couple of minutes the lead hardens and the mould is removed from the vice with a pair of tongs. The two halves of the mould are split open to expose the freshly made sinker which is then placed in a bucket of water positioned well away from the working area.

The process is repeated until all the molten lead is used. It's advisable not to heat the melting pot completely dry. As soon as it starts to get low, top it up with a fresh lot of lead. Any sinkers you find on the beach can be melted down in this manner.

It must be stressed again that this is NOT a job which should be tackled by a youngster. Molten lead is potentially lethal.

Transporting bait

The average-size cool box with a couple of ice packs in the bottom should hold about four shallow trays of worms, each lined with damp hessian sacking. The same method is suitable for crabs but they benefit from being covered with a layer of weed or another damp piece of sack. About 50 worms per tray is the maximum loading.

White ragworm are more of a problem. I use two litre ice cream tubs with an inch of coral sand in the base and place no more than ten snakes in each. The tubs are filled with fresh seawater until it is about .25in above the sand layer. The containers can be stacked one inside the other.

Frozen bait

Four ice packs in a cool box is the rule for frozen baits which must travel long distances. Place the cool box in the freezer at least two days before your journey to eliminate any warm air pockets.

Filleting fish

If you take a few fish home for the table it makes sense to learn the correct filleting techniques to remove as much flesh as possible.

Round fish

For round fish like cod, bass and pollack, make a diagonal cut just behind the gills right down to the backbone. Slide the knife along the backbone starting at the bottom of the initial cut, slowly working down the entire fish until the whole fillet is removed. Repeat the process on the other side.

With smaller fish up to 3lb, it is worth slicing them into cutlets to eliminate waste. Lay the fish on a flat surface, cut off the tail and slice right through the fish in a series of manageable sized cutlets of approximately 1.5in.

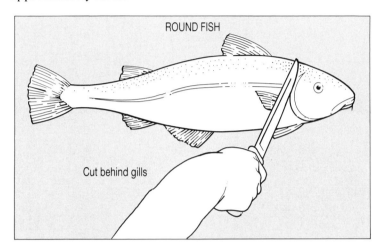

ROUND FISH

Cut behind gills

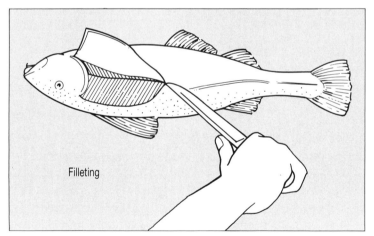

Filleting

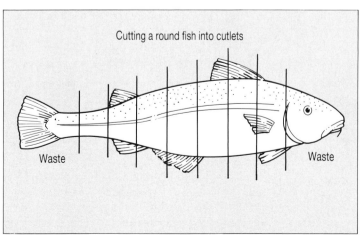

Cutting a round fish into cutlets

Waste   Waste

Flatfish

I do not follow the usual procedure for filleting flatfish. I prefer to cut down the entire length of the backbone on either side of the fish. It is then very easy to remove the four fillets.

With skate, cut off the the two wings whole as in the diagram below. These are then cut into smaller strips.

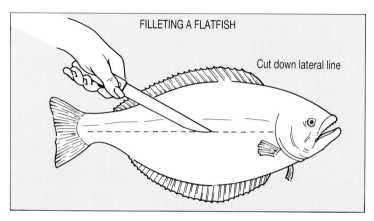

FILLETING A FLATFISH

Cut down lateral line

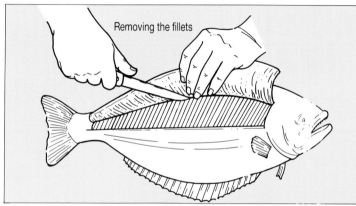

Removing the fillets

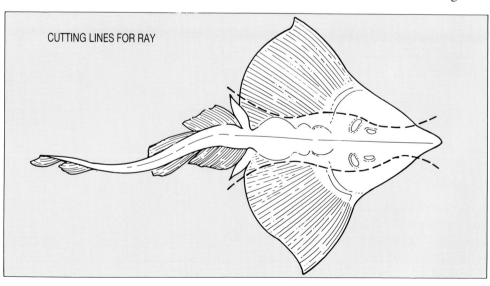

CUTTING LINES FOR RAY

Safety on the seashore

The golden rule is to inform a member of the family or friends where you are going and the time you expect to return. This applies whether you are going fishing or bait digging.

Where there's vast expanses of tidal mud or sand, carry a small compass and a whistle. A sudden fog can make you lose your bearings and possibly walk straight into danger. Encircling tides which flood through deep gullies and cut off your escape route are another hazard.

Carry a spare torch when nightfishing in case your main light cuts out and watch out for rusty nails in driftwood or broken glass. Most accidents on the seashore can be prevented by taking commonsense precautions.

Dangerous fish

Weevers

The weever only grows to around 6in and looks innocent enough but it could land you in hospital. They are found on shallow, sandy beaches and have extremely sharp, venomous spines on the dorsal. The slightest scratch from one of these spines will cause painful, unsightly swelling and excruciating pain.

There is no known antidote although the

pain is often relieved by soaking the infected area in hot water. Handle weevers with thick gloves and a towel.

Dragonets

Dragonets are another problem fish. Protruding from each gill cover are sharp bones which are capable of inflicting a very deep wound.

Stingrays

Then there is the stingray, of course. Many anglers believe that the long, whippy tail presents danger but the real hazard is a very sharp, spear-like spine –sometimes as long as 6in – at the base of the tail. I have seen this spine penetrate half-inch ply on a dinghy. If you are unfortunate enough to get wounded by a stingray, hospital treatment is advisable.

Huss family

Dogfish and other members of the huss family have skin like coarse sandpaper and should be handled with gloves. With small fish, you can hold the head and tail together but larger specimens like smoothhound and bull huss are best gripped by the tail and dorsal.

Sea scorpion

The sea scorpion which grows to just 8oz has several sharp spines and thorny outcrops on its head. These are not poisonous but wounds might turn sceptic.

Conger and angler fish

Big conger and angler fish possess rows of fearsome teeth capable of inflicting very serious injury. I always use long handled pliers to remove the hook from a conger, just to be on the safe side.

Rays

Rays, on the other hand, grind up their food and if your fingers become trapped in the mouth you will have a heck of a job getting them out. A bar is normally needed to force the jaw open.

Conservation

Every angler has a responsibility to help conserve fish for future generations. All fish under Ministry minimum sizes must go back immediately. And there's no point in killing the likes of wrasse, stingray and garfish which make for very poor eating. Only dig sufficient bait for your needs.

Sea anglers' code

Always follow the code drawn up by the National Federation of Sea Anglers which represents more than 500 clubs. The main points are as follows:
1. Observe local byelaws except where they are contrary to rights under Magna Carta.
2. Gather only what you need to ensure future supplies of bait.
3. Backfill all holes and maintain the inter-tidal habitat.
4. Replace rocks and stones the correct way up to preserve the food chain.
5. Do not dig around moorings, slipways and sea walls.
6. Be aware of local hazards like soft mud, quicksands, tidal flows, fog and adverse weather.
7. Do not disturb nesting birds.
8. Take all litter home.
9. Tell someone where you intend to dig for bait.

One point not covered by the code is the taking of small and immature worms which puts the very existence of the beds at risk. The importance of sticking to these rules cannot be emphasised enough. Our freedom to fish and dig baiton any beach depends on it.

Club membership

A strong, united network of angling clubs is the most effective way of defending and promoting the sport's interests at local

The fierce looking dragonet is regularly caught on rod and line.

and national level. I'd like to see every sea angler enlist with his local club to provide the strongest possible organisational structure. An average subscription fee of £5 seems a small price to pay for the protection of our sport. End of political message!

There are considerable benefits in signing up as the flow of useful information in club circles will steer you to the most productive marks and keep you informed of current sporting trends.

The 500 plus clubs in membership of the National Federation of Sea Anglers are split into nine regions and are primarily responsible for dealing with such issues as bait digging restrictions and conservation issues.

Who knows what lies at the end of the breakwater – shorefishing is full of surprises.

How to claim a record

The National Anglers' Council runs the British Record (rod-caught) Fish Committee which is the recognised body for judging and awarding national bests in boat and shore categories. If you are fortunate enough to beach a record-breaker then telephone the BRFC

secretary immediately for advice on identification procedures. The address of the Committee is 11 Cowgate, Peterborough PE1 1LZ (telephone 0733-54084).

The fish must be played by the captor alone on rod and line but assistance with gaffing or netting is permitted as long as the helper does not touch any part of the tackle other than the leader. A weights and measures certificate must be produced for the scales used to record the fish in front of two independent witnesses.

To avoid any possible misunderstandings, make a point of investing in a telephone call to the BRFC's office. It is the only sure way of avoiding slip-ups in the weighing and identification. Claims for fish caught in Eire should be made to the Irish Specimen Fish Committee, Balnagowan, Mobhi Boreen, Glasnevin, Dublin 9.

World records

World-record marine fish are the concern of the International Game Fish Association, Holiday Inn Arcade, 3000E, Las Olas Boulevard, Fort Lauderdale, Florida 33316, USA.

Shark candidates should approach the Shark Angling Club of Great Britain based at Looe in Cornwall.

Insurance

I would advise every angler to make sure he has adequate cover to meet third party liability in the event of an accident on the beach. My understanding is that many household and contents policies provide this sort of cover but get the policy checked by an expert.

The NFSA take out a blanket third party liability policy on behalf of all their affiliated clubs. Accidental injury and damage to property are covered, although the first £50 of any claim must be paid by the club member. Clubs and individuals who organise Open events are advised to take out an extra policy to cover non-affiliated

INDEX

Figures in italics refer to illustrations